MORE

AMAZING

but true

MORMON
STORIES

MORE AMAZING but true MORMON STORIES

JOAN OVIATT

ISBN 13: 978-0-88290-578-5

Published by Horizon Publishers, an imprint of Cedar Fort, Inc.,
2373 W. 700 S., Springville, UT, 84663
Distributed by Cedar Fort, Inc. www.cedarfort.com

Cover design by Angela Olsen
Cover design © 2008 by Lyle Mortimer

Printed in the United States of America

10 9 8 7 6 5 4 3 2 1

Printed on acid-free paper

Contents

About the Author   7
Do Your Homework!   9
The Unpopular Girl 11
Santa Claus Versus the Ku Klux Klan 14
That Face 16
An Effective Speaker 17
Ephraim Humor 18
Lively Spirits 21
The Bear Lake Monsters 23
Monument to Dreams 27
The Unusual Speaker 29
Musical Identity 31
Hero for Peace 34
Super Star 36
The Mysterious Substance 40
Playing with Guns 42
A Wild West Tale 44
Reverse Psychology 46
A New Trend 48
Healing Stones 49
The Red Ghost 51
The Man Who Got Coal for Christmas 54
The Kid Who Drove Cars 56
Tale of the Dead Coyote 58
The Death Prophecy 61
Put Them Right 62

Half a World Away   64
The Cooperative Choir   67
A Modern Woman   69
The Runaway   72
Evicted From Their Town   75
The Gospel According to Gibson   77
Parley and the Bull Dog   82
Rebel with a Cause   85
The Promised Babe   88
Frontier M.D.   90
Emergency at the Virgin Ditch   92
The Big Mine   94
The Non-Mormon Who Saved Nauvoo   96
The Unloved Woman   99
Ghost in the Picture   109
Heavenly First Aid   111
The Naughty Boy   113
Maori Prophecy   115
Test of Brotherhood   118
Japanese Land   120
Taters and Testimony   123
Attack of the Dead Cat   126
Tale of the Buckskin Pants   128
Escape from Liberty   131
No Place to Lose a Cow   134
He Spoke with Humor and Persuasive Power   137
J. Golden and the Brass Band   141
He Couldn't Be Broken   144
The Iceberg   148
The Cripple Who Wanted to Serve a Mission   150
Bibliography   153

About the Author

Joan Oviatt attended college in California, Hawaii, and Utah, receiving a Master of Arts degree from Brigham Young University in 1978. She has garnered numerous awards in writing, music, art, acting, directing and academics, and was named to Outstanding Young Women of America by the BYU Alumni Association.

Joan won the BYU Sesquicentennial Playwriting Contest with her play, "The Field is White." In the Mormon Festival of Arts competition she won first place in the playwriting area for her musical play "Portrait of a Convert." Her play "Can't Stand Still" ran the full summer, with 44 performances at Utah's Sundance Theatre. As a performer she has appeared in more than 60 stage plays and films.

Joan is a published novelist and lyricist as well as a playwright. *More Amazing But True Mormon Stories* is her seventh book. It is preceded by *Amazing But True Mormon Stories*, *Popular Girls*, *The One Game*, *Mormon Mind Puzzlers*, *Master Anthology of Scripture Riddles*, and *Episodes of Mormon Mystery*. Articles published by the *New Era* and the *Ensign* are also in her portfolio of published writings.

Joan currently resides in Salt Lake City where she works as a freelance writer and researcher.

Do Your Homework!

The kid grew up in Utah and Idaho. He loved studying, especially anything mechanical or having to do with electricity. He was even familiar with Einstein's theory of relativity. And he loved to do homework. He loved homework so much that he did homework that wasn't assigned to him. He made up his own assignments and showed them to his teachers.

The kid had a dream. He was going to invent something that would change the world. He was going to invent something that would end illiteracy. He was going to invent something that would bring world peace by communicating with, and bringing closer together, the nations of the world.

At age twenty-one, the young man had his invention, though in a very rough stage. When he demonstrated it on September 7, 1927, it made the news. Scientists and businessmen came to see him. In an effort to secure financing to develop his invention, he trustingly demonstrated it for fellow inventors, only to find some of them copying his invention and trying to pass off his developments as their own. He spent many years in courts trying to defend his patents.

In trying to defend his claim as first innovator of the invention, the young man had to take on the incredibly powerful Radio Corporation of America. His plight seemed almost hopeless, but then someone showed up in court to testify for the young man. It was his high school teacher. The teacher had with him a sample of the young man's homework. The homework proved that the young man had conceived the invention before the corporate giant.

Today, a statue of the man, grandson of Mormon pioneers and a pioneer himself, stands in the U.S. Capitol building in Washington, D.C. The United States honored him on a first-class postage stamp in 1983. He is now recognized and revered, even though that was not always so in his lifetime. His invention has been revised, improved, developed, advanced by many. Unfortunately, the use which the inventor envisioned for his invention was never realized. But no one can deny that Philo T. Farnsworth, the inventor of the first television camera and father of the electronic television, truly has changed the world.

The Unpopular Girl

Mamie was born in 1870 to a pioneer family. Her older sister was pretty, but she was plain. As Mamie wrote in her journal, "Unlike Minnie I was very plain and unattractive, with small 'squinty' blue eyes, straight, coarse, dull-colored hair, with a 'cowlick' so it never would part in the middle. Thus I started life handicapped from the beginning, but Mother would apologize for my looks by saying, 'Well, she has a sunny disposition anyway,' and for that one endowment I have been very grateful, as it has been a greater asset then looks possibly could be."

As a child Mamie became the butt of jokes because of her big feet. Her father treated her much like a boy and gave her coarse chores to do on the pioneer farm. As early as eleven years of age, Mamie was driving teams of horses to get loads of hay to market. When her beloved sister Minnie died, Mamie's life was radically changed. As the oldest surviving of ten children, and having a mother in delicate health, Mamie shouldered a work load that precluded most childhood activities. Hers was a life filled with work. She labored from morning to night. Even when she had the chance to sit down she had knitting needles in her hands to make stockings.

During the winters Mamie went to school. She was always outspoken. One time she told her class that she was "sweet sixteen and never been kissed!" Her classmates laughed and teased her about it for years. She finally met a boy in school who liked her. They were inseparable. He went on a mission and she waited for him. She dated no one else. He came back and again they were inseparable. He went to Provo to attend Brigham Young Academy and never returned—he met a girl there he liked better and married her.

Mamie's family moved to a ranch closer to Kanab, Utah. There she became the subject of controversy. In a town council meeting, an old man, Charles Cram, charged that Mamie was riding about the streets of Kanab astraddle a horse and she was wearing divided skirts. Something had to be done about her. This caused some hilarity at the council meeting. The thought of Mamie sitting side saddle with flowing skirts made them laugh. They all knew she was a hard-working ranch girl who wore what suited the work. And, after all, these were modern times—the late 1800's. Mr. Cram was told he'd just awakened from a Rip Van Winkle sleep.

In 1890, Mamie went to Latter-day Saints College in Salt Lake City to complete her education. She was exposed to many social events that increased her appreciation of finer things. The socially inadequate girl began to bloom. Upon graduation from the college, Mamie was chosen to give the commencement address on behalf of the women students. In her talk she said, "The young ladies of this institution (I am proud to say) stand on an equal plane with the young men and receive from them the respect which equals demand. Sex with us is no distinction. If there is anything to be performed and a lady is capable, the fact of her being 'fair' does not deter her. Her opinion is expressed and sanctioned, her testimony borne and sustained the same as that of her brethren."

After graduation, Mamie moved to St. George where she worked as a clerk at a general store. She did everything from measuring silk to hefting and hauling feed bags and butchering.

When Utah achieved statehood in 1896, women were finally allowed to run for public office. Mamie ran a tough campaign for county clerk against a male opponent. She won, becoming the first woman to be elected county clerk in Utah. She was twenty-six and still single. In spite of her lack of physical charms, most everyone knew and liked her.

In 1900, at age thirty, Mamie married Thomas Chamberlain and soon gave birth to two sons. She still worked at the general store, and also kept house and raised her family. She taught Sunday School and served as superintendent of her ward religion class.

A history-making election occurred in November of 1911. Against her desires, Mamie was nominated for mayor of Kanab, Utah. She was nominated under her assumed professional name, Mary Woolley Howard. The nomination was an astonishing thing for its era. Never had a woman served as mayor west of the Rockies.[1] But Mamie was now a popular woman. The hesitant candidate received overwhelming support from the citizenry. Even more amazing, an all-woman town council was elected. Tamar Stewart Hamblin was elected clerk, Luella Atkin McAllister was elected treasurer, Blanche Robinson Hamblin and Ada Pratt Seegmiller rounded out the council. The election was so unusual for its time that it was reported in newspapers even in London.

All over Utah women were being elected to positions as treasurers, auditors and recorders. But Kanab was the first town in Utah, and the first town in the West, to have a woman mayor and an all-female city council.

Mamie Woolley Howard/Chamberlain, serving as mayor by popular vote, instigated significant public works to beautify Kanab and to prevent flood damage. Many considered her the best mayor they'd ever had. She served two years and after leaving the office she continued her civic work.

Mary Elizabeth Woolley Chamberlain, "Mamie," died in 1953 at the age of eighty-three. She will be remembered for many things, including her popular election as first lady mayor in the West.

---

[1] In fact, only twice before had a woman served as mayor of an American town. Susanna Medora Salter was elected mayor of Argonia, Kansas, in 1887. Mary Lowman was elected mayor of Oskaloosa, Kansas, in 1888, along with a female city council.

14

Santa Claus Versus the Ku Klux Klan

T he Ku Klux Klan was a powerful organization in the United States in the 1920's. Dressing in robes with hoods that hid their faces, Klan members engaged in acts of punishment against those with different ideas or heritages than their own. Espousing bigotry and vigilantism, the Klan found followers in many states. It found followers in Utah, though not many. To gain power it courted the favor of The Church of Jesus Christ of Latter-day Saints, but was rebuffed. Elder Charles W. Nibley, Presiding Bishop of the Church at the time, denounced the organization in October conference in 1922. President Heber J. Grant refused requested meetings with Klan officials. In October conference in 1924, George Albert Smith spoke out against secret organizations like the Klan. He said that no one could be a faithful member of the Church who affiliated with such groups.

In 1925, the Klan sponsored a conference of their own to coincide with April LDS Conference. They set crosses afire on Ensign Peak. Even in a time of many societal prejudices, the Klan was too extreme for the citizenry of Salt Lake City. The city commission, searching for a way to control the masked fanatics, passed an anti-mask ordinance. If the Klan wanted to practice their constitutionally guaranteed right of free speech, hate-filled as it was, they would have to do it without their faces covered.

In December, 1925, the Klansmen thought to overturn the anti-mask ordinance by a simple ploy. They would face down

Santa Claus. But, as any child can tell you, you can't defeat Santa Claus.

In the city council meeting, council members said that it had been brought to their attention by Klan officials that the false beards worn in public by Santa Clauses violated the municipal anti-mask ordinance. The issue was debated. To guarantee equal rights, the city council was forced to outlaw Santa Clauses. An unpopular order was sent to police to enforce the anti-mask ordinance on everyone, including Santa Claus. The Ogden city council was forced to take the same action.

On Christmas, one Santa Claus defiantly appeared on the streets of Ogden, but no policeman could be found to arrest him. The "Unmasking of Santa" in Salt Lake City appeared in the *New York Times* on December 24. It was the only time an incident involving the Utah Klan was reported on the national wire service.

Instead of making people sympathetic to the rights of the Klan, it subjected them to popular ridicule for attacking a symbol of goodwill. They were blamed for driving Santa from the streets. The Klan were largely disliked and shortly after disappeared from any significant activity in Salt Lake City or Utah.

The Klan disappeared but Santa did not. Santa Clauses were gradually permitted in public again. The anti-mask ordinance was finally repealed after it was discovered to be still on the books in the 1970's.

That Face

Colleen was on a plane trip. The flight attendants were serving coffee. A stewardess she had never met before came up to Colleen and, instead of asking her if she wanted coffee, said, "I'll be glad to make you a cup of Postum if you have brought your can along with you."

People knew Colleen's face and knew what she stood for. Colleen was an actress, but that's not what had brought her fame. Colleen was a pianist, but that's not what she was famous for. Colleen was a competitive swimmer, but that's not what she was famous for. Her brother Mel was a professional basketball player, but that's not how they knew her face.

Colleen appeared on television and radio. She attended sporting events, festivals, and rode in parades. she was interviewed by newspapers and never lost the chance to promote good homes, religious values, the Word of Wisdom. She crisscrossed the country and traveled to other countries promoting wholesome values and, in doing so, obtained positive publicity for the Church.

The director of the Miss America Pageant said that Colleen, Miss America 1952, was the busiest and most popular of all Miss Americas. Colleen Kay Hutchins was the first Mormon Miss America.

An Effective Speaker

He served as head of Brigham Young University for twenty-one years, first as acting principal at the turn of the century, then as president from 1904 to 1921. He oversaw its growth from a small institution to a respected full-size university. More important to him than educational goals, however, was the development of character in his students. He presided over frequent student devotionals.

On one occasion a poor student left his watch in his gym locker when he went to gym class. When he returned, the watch was gone. The incident was reported to him.

At the student devotional the next morning, the President said, "Whoever took that watch will find no enjoyment from it. Each tick will say to you 'Thief! Thief! Thief! Thief! Thief!' To the guilty person I say, it is not too late to change. You have made a grave mistake. Here is a chance to correct it, quickly. I'm going to leave the door to my office open tonight when I go home. Tomorrow morning, when I come to work, I expect to find that watch on my desk."

Early the next morning President George H. Brimhall walked into his office. There, on his desk, were three watches.

Ephraim Humor

The first language into which the Book of Mormon was translated was English. But the second language was Danish. The Book of Mormon was translated in Copenhagen, Denmark, headquarters of the Scandinavian Mission, in 1851. Between 1850 and 1930, 26,656 people were baptized in Denmark.

In those early years of the Church, most of the Danish members emigrated to Utah to be near the Church center. They came by wagon, handcart and train. They settled throughout the Utah territory. In communities such as Ephraim and Manti, the majority were Danes. To become assimilated into their new country they learned English. The combination of their new country and new religion with their old ways created a culture which was unique.

Scandinavian genealogy is unique. In Denmark, if a man named Hans had children, all the children had the last name of Hanson or Hansen. If one of those children was named Neils Hanson, his children would all have the last name of Neilson or Neilsen. Last names were based on father's first names.

The Danish Saints, on settling Utah, began to use the English system of surnames. Some communities were primarily made up of a dozen or so surnames: Christensen, Madsen, Olsen, Jensen, Bensen, Andersen, etc.

One story is told of a Sunday when Sacrament meeting was ending. The bishop stood up and, without thinking, asked, "Brodder Peterson, vil you please come up to de stand und offer de closing prayer?" Twenty-three Brother Petersons rose to their feet. "I mean," the bishop corrected himself, "Brodder Peter Peterson." Seven Brother Petersons sat down.

To clarify the identities of residents, Danish communities such as Ephraim invented nicknames. Nicknames could be based on something a person said or did or looked like. Examples were Andrew "Ah-Ha" Anderson, "Otto By-yingo" Anderson, "Bulldog" Anderson, "Stinkbug" Anderson, Soren "Chickenheart" Anderson, "Yens Fiddler" Jensen, "Sarah Fat" Peterson, "Long Soren" Sorenson, Bert "Fiddlesticks" Christensen, "Crazy" Poulsen, "Pete Pig-killer" Hansen, "Red Whiskers" Olsen, "Perty Pete" Larsen.

The Danish Saints experienced the same hardships as other pioneers. Maren Kirstine Nielson recorded, "The food problem was harder to solve, especially in the winter. We tired of our evening meal of boiled wheat and wild jack rabbit. Once one of our boys, Lauritz, was asked to say the blessing on the meal. He did, with the following verse he had made up:

> Rabbit young, Rabbit old,
> Rabbit hot, Rabbit cold,
> Rabbit tender and Rabbit tough.
> Oh please, Dear Lord,
> We've had enough.

Struggling in a new country with a complex language, the Danish Saints had their share of humorous lapses. In Ephraim, the stories of these lapses were told and retold. Proud of their heritage of humor, Ephraim developed a reputation as "the town that laughs at itself." In a testimony meeting "Pete Friday" Petersen is said to have said: "Brodders and sisters, der comes a great comfort from family prayers. No matter where I am—when I am out in de valley wit de sheep, all alone—when I am in de mountains wit de cattle, all alone—when I am riding in de desert, all alone by myself—I alvays kneels down and has my family prayers."

Another good old brother stood in testimony meeting and said, "Brodders and sisters, ven I come to dis country I had noddings—no house, no barn, no vife, no children, no clothes, no cows, no noddings. Now I have all dese tings, und my cellar is full of milk an cream an fruit an yam an yelly, an brodders and sisters, I vant to bear my testimony dat de Lord has had his finger in it all."

Folklorist Thomas Cheney recorded the following story from the Scandinavian settlers of Utah. When Brother Christensen, an original pioneer of Ephraim, died, a brother who loved to philosophize was asked to be a speaker at the funeral. The eulogy for the deceased went like this: "De Bishop haf asked me to spake de funeral sermon of Brodder Christensen und I don't know anyting dat vill gif me more joy. It vas yust a few veeks ago dat he vas galavanting around here full of vim and vitality, un now all dat is before us is yust de old carcass—de shell as it var; de nut has gone. Ven he vas sick it seemed for a little vile dat he vould recruit but he suffered a prolapse un vent to his happy hunting ground ver der is no pain or tears, or Vord of Visdom.

"Brodder Christensen vas a patriotic man un many a time he has sung de 'Star Spangled Flag,' und many times haf I heard him recite dos beautiful vords from dat grand old Patriarch George Vashington: Breathes der de man vit soul so dead, Who never said to himself, Dis is my own, my native land, Veder he vas born here or in Denmark?

"Und alvays he vas a minute man un a true soldier. I feel it an honor to add a boo-ket to de character of dis fine old veterinary.

"He didn't know a great deal about dis vorld. He tought dat Henry Clay var a kind of adobe mud, but he var spiritually minded, und more dan vonce he testified dat he had peered into the great behind.

"He vas a very gud recitation speaker, und oh how I like to hear him recitation dat poem 'Oh Death, var is thy stinger.'

"Und so considering all de vonderful characteristics of dis Brodder I tink ve can take him out un have him interned in dat barn from vich no traveling man returns. He have given me a testimony of de great principle—de immortality of de soul, vich he had practiced all his life. Un now I close in the name of de Holy Ghost, Amen."

The Ephraimites prize their heritage, but, as one old Dane said with a twinkle, "Half de lies dey tells about us, isn't true.

Lively Spirits

In his autobiography, he wrote: "One incident that impressed itself upon me, physically as well as mentally, was the accidental scalding of my head by a hired help, a girl, who carelessly wrung a hot dishcloth over me as I sat upon the doorstep of our humble cabin home. They say I was rather hotheaded when a boy. I certainly was on that occasion.

As a child, Orson attended school in Salt Lake City. President Brigham Young and other church and civil authorities would visit the school. "I well remember one of their visits," wrote Orson. "Overawed by such august onlookers, several of the girls fainted while reading, and one or two of the boys wept aloud. Fearing a similar fate, I braced myself for the ordeal and shouted out my piece, 'The Suicidal Cat,' with all the lung power at my command. To my huge surprise, it established my reputation as a comic speaker."

Orson grew up with an artistic temperament. He did poorly in school in math, but he enjoyed poetry and theatrics. As a teenager he got work in railroad construction. Later he worked as a driver, clerk, salesman, and teacher. He was generally serious, sometimes melancholy, but also humorously inclined.

Orson was made a bishop at twenty-three years of age, even though he was unmarried—an unheard of thing for a Mormon bishop. He tried his hand at politics, being elected a city councilman, a party delegate, and a state senator at different times. In 1884, he was appointed city treasurer for Salt Lake City. One day a lady, demanding attention, disrupted the monotony of the office work. Even though it was city hall, she came demanding religious assistance from young Orson, who was bishop of the 18th Ward.

As Orson recorded:

"I want to get up into the Eighteenth Ward," she said.

"What for?"

"I'm troubled with evil spirits, and I believe they would leave me if I got up into the Eighteenth Ward."

"Where do you live now?"

"In the Thirteenth Ward."

"How do you know they are evil spirits?"

"Oh, they shriek out in the night, and are like fire in my bed. They jerk the pillow out from under me."

"Have you been to your Bishop about it?"

"Yes, Bishop Atwood says he can't do anything for me."

"Have you been to the President of the Stake?"

"Yes, I've seen Angus M. Cannon."

"What did he say?"

"He told me to tell Bishop Atwood to fast and pray and cast 'em out."

"And what did the Bishop say to that?"

"He said, 'Go back to Angus M. Cannon and tell *him* to fast and pray and cast 'em out.' So I want to leave that ward, and get up into the Eighteenth."

By this time quite a group of City employees had gathered round, among them my uncle, droll Solomon Kimball, who was Janitor and Jailer. He was also a zealous member of the Eighteenth Ward, and thought things were done a little more thoroughly up there than anywhere else. Fixing his eye on my strange visitor he said, "You say they jerk the pillow out from under you?"

"Yes."

"You come up into the Eighteenth Ward and they'll jerk the whole bed out from under you!"

That was enough. Without further ado she went her way, seemingly resolved, like Hamlet, rather to bear the evil spirit she had, than "fly to others" that she "knew not of."

Orson F. Whitney became a recognized author, historian and poet. In 1906, he was made a member of the Council of Twelve

Apostles, though he said he was intimidated by the importance of that calling and always preferred the role of bishop.

The Bear Lake Monsters

Rumors about monsters in Bear Lake, on the Utah-Idaho border, have floated about ever since the area was settled by Mormon pioneers. One of the first and best written accounts was reported by Joseph C. Rich. Datelined "Paris, Rich County, Utah, July 27, 1868," the article appeared in the *Deseret Evening News* on August 3, 1868:

All lakes, caves and dens have their legendary histories. Tradition loves to throw her magic wand over beautiful dells and lakes and people them with fairies, giants and monsters of various kinds. Bear Lake has also its monster tale to tell, and when I have told it, I will leave you to judge whether or not it is merely tradition.

The Indians say there is a monster animal which lives in the Lake that has captured and carried away Indians while in the Lake swimming; but they say it has not been seen by them for many years, not since the buffalo inhabited the valley. They represent it as being of the serpent kind, but having legs about eighteen inches long on which they sometimes crawl out of the water a short distance on the shore. They also say it spurts water upwards out of its mouth.

Since the settlement of this valley several persons have reported seeing a huge animal of some kind that they could not describe; but such persons have generally been alone when they saw it, and little credence has been attached to the matter, and until this summer the "monster question" had about died out.

About three weeks ago Mr. S. M. Johnson, who lives on the east side of the lake at the place called South Eden was going to the Round Valley settlement, six miles to the South of this place when about half way he saw something in the lake which at the time, he thought to be a drowned person. The road being close to the water's edge he went to the beach. The waves were running pretty high. He thought it would soon wash into shore. In a few minutes two or three feet of some kind of an animal that he had never seen before were raised out of the water. He did not see the body, only the head and what he supposed to be part of the neck. It had ears or bunches on the side of its head nearly as large as a pint cup. The waves at times would dash over its head, when it would throw water from its mouth or nose. It did not drift landward, but appeared stationary, with the exception of turning its head. Mr. Johnson thought a portion of the body must lie on the bottom of the lake or it would have drifted with the action of the water. This is Mr. Johnson's version as he told me.

The next day an animal of a monster kind was seen near the same place by a man and three women, who said it was swimming when they first saw it. They described it as being very large, and said it swam much faster than a horse could run on land. These recent testimonies again revived the 'monster question.' Those who had seen it before repeated their accounts. Many people began to think there was something to the story.

On Sunday last N. C. Davis and Allen Davis, of St. Charles, and Thomas Slight and J. Collings of Paris, with six women, were returning from Fish Haven. When about half way to St. Charles, their attention was suddenly attracted to a peculiar motion or wave in the water, about three miles distant. The lake was not rough, only a little disturbed by a light wind. Mr. Slight says he distinctly saw the sides of a very large animal that he would suppose to be not less than ninety feet in length. Mr. Davis didn't think he saw any part of the body, but is positive it must have been not less than forty feet in length, judging by the wave it rolled upon both sides of it as it swam, and the wake it left in the rear. It was going South, and all agreed that it swam with incredible speed. Mr. Davis says he never saw a locomotive travel faster, and thinks it made a mile a minute, easy. In a few minutes after the discovery of the first creature, a second one followed in its wake; but it seemed much smaller, appearing to Mr. Slight about the size of a horse. This was followed by another small one. In all, the large one and six small ones were counted as they swam southward out of sight.

One of the creatures before disappearing made a sudden turn to the west, a short distance; then back to its former track. At this turn Mr. Slight says he could distinctly see it was of a brownish color. They could judge somewhat of their speed by observing known distances on the other side of the lake, and all agree that the velocity with which they propelled themselves through the water was astonishing. They estimated the waves that rolled up in front and on each side of them as being three feet high from where they stood. This is substantially their statement as they told me. Davis and Slight are prominent men, well known in this country, and all of them are reliable persons whose veracity is undoubted. I have no doubt they would be willing to make affidavits to their statement.

There you have the monster story so far as completed, but I hope it will be concluded by the capture of one sometime. If so large an animal exists in this altitude and in so small a lake, what could it be? Is it fish, flesh or serpent, amphibious and fabulous or a great big fish, or what is it? We have hopes of someday seeing it, if it really exists, and I have no reason to doubt the above statements. Here is an excellent opportunity for some entertainment company, if they can only catch one. Already some of our settlers talk of forming a joint stock arrangement.

So went Joseph C. Rich's account. People seemed to see more and more of the monsters, especially after the article appeared. Reports came in of varying descriptions: A scaly reptile, a serpent-like form, a head like an otter's, a head like a cow.

Educated men speculated how a species of gigantic swimming lizard-like creatures living in Lake Bonneville (which encompassed much of Utah) during the Mesozoic period might have survived in the Bear Lake waters when the seas receded.

Because respectable people claimed to have seen the creatures, others tried to contrive reasonable explanations: A wave of carp which swim Bear Lake in such concentrated numbers that they have been known to boil the water in a half-mile roll, or two elk swimming together, as they sometimes do, giving an appearance of length and coil at a distance.

The man who first picked up on the Indian legend and embellished it with his own witnesses and descriptions, Joseph C. Rich, continued to keep the stir going by sending in reports for another twenty years. But there was something about Joseph Rich which most newspaper readers and monster enthusiasts didn't know. Joseph was the son of Apostle Charles C. Rich of the Council of Twelve. Unlike his father, Joseph was an inveterate practical joker and more than once his father had to take him to task.

Joseph, at the time of the monsters, was in love with a young woman. They lived in a small settlement in Idaho. The young woman did not like living there and determined to go to the city. Joseph decided he had to do something. He had to do something that would bring thousands of visitors to the area and provide the crowds and company the young woman yearned for. Others helped him in his plot. He invented the Bear Lake Monsters. In his articles to the *Deseret News* he incorporated realistic-sounding reporting. He had reliable witnesses. However, those 'witnesses'—S.M. Johnson, N.C. Davis, Thomas Slight, J. Collings, and all the others—were made up. There were no such "reliable" witnesses.

Joseph's invention worked half way. Thousands came to look for the monsters. Unfortunately, the young woman left anyway. But the power of suggestion is great, and even today someone occasionally claims to see a Bear Lake monster.

Monument to Dreams

J ens Moller Borglum was born in Denmark in 1837. In 1856, the idealistic young man found The Church of Jesus Christ of Latter-day Saints and was baptized. He served as a missionary in his native land for seven years without purse or scrip, subsisting on meager hospitalities and gospel ideals. In 1864, he left Copenhagen with another group of Danish Saints. They were filled with dreams, not only of a Zion, but of the promised land of America.

In 1864, Moller arrived in Salt Lake City. Shortly after his arrival he married a Danish sister, Christiane. They moved to the Bear Lake Valley in southeastern Idaho to establish a place for themselves in this new land. Moller had several children, including a son born in St. Charles, Idaho. His name was Gutzon.

Moller was a skilled carpenter and woodworker, but he found little work. The family moved to Ogden. The opportunities there were still not what they desired. Moller felt unfulfilled.

Relatives who settled in Nebraska told the family to come there, so in 1869, Moller and his family moved to Omaha. Moller went to medical school, returning to become a frontier doctor in Nebraska. He was not a rich doctor, for he worked with many poor people who couldn't afford his services. But whether his patients were rich or poor, the kindly doctor served them just the same.

The good doctor had a lifelong passion for genealogy which he continued to share with his Utah relatives. The family remained friendly to the Church, though they drifted from activity. Some of the family joined the Roman Catholic faith. The doctor never joined another faith, preferring to keep his own independent beliefs.

Moller raised his children with his ideals. One child became a doctor, another a musician, another an inventor, another an artist.

But family life was not perfect. His son Gutzon was a troubled youth who ran away. To deal with him, Gutzon was sent to a Catholic boarding school in Kansas.

Dr. Jens Moller Borglum died in 1909, but his son Gutzon grew to adopt his father's ideals. He became an artist. He was not a widely acclaimed artist, but he had a story he wanted to share. He wanted to tell the story of a young nation born of inspiration, compassion, struggle and foresight. His desire was to portray the dreams and ambitions, accomplishments and ideals, that shaped his family's adopted country. He wanted to tell the story of the United States of America.

In 1927, he was offered the opportunity to create a monument. Gutzon died in 1941, leaving his son Lincoln to finish the major work of his lifetime.

Gutzon Borglum's name is not known by many, but his work of art is known throughout the world. It is visited by a million people a year. Carved on the side of a mountain, his story in stone is called Mount Rushmore.

The Unusual Speaker

It was April conference, 1950. President George Albert Smith was presiding. David O. McKay was conducting. President Smith recognized an elderly man sitting in the Tabernacle congregation and felt impressed that he should speak. President McKay called the man to the podium.

The man called on the spur of the moment to speak was named Samuel. He was not a general authority, he was not even a stake president. He was not a politician. He was not a leader of business or industry. In fact, Samuel was poor. He barely saved enough for the trip to conference. Much of what he earned in his life was spent to help the missionaries and to support the growth of the Church.

Samuel was not an influential writer. In fact, Samuel could not read or write. Yet now he stood before the leadership of the Church, his eloquent words being broadcast by radio to thousands.

Samuel could quote the scriptures because, with his great mind, he'd memorized most of the standard works. And he could speak eloquently because he had much practice speaking on behalf of justice and humanity before representatives of the U.S. government. Now, in conference, he told his story.

Samuel lived in a log cabin in a poor community in the woods of South Carolina. In 1883, when Samuel was fifteen years old, two Mormon missionaries, Elders Henry Miller and C. E. Robinson, came upon the community. In their missionary journeys they had been tarred and feathered, beaten, mobbed and pelted with stones. Yet when they entered Samuel's town, they were peacefully greeted and welcomed into homes. Samuel had a job working for twenty-five cents a day. Those wages supported his family. When the missionaries came, he fed them as well. There was not enough room in his cabin to fit everyone, so Samuel gave the missionaries his bed while he slept outside on the ground.

The missionaries preached to the people of the community. When mobs from outside the community threatened, the citizens of the town protected the missionaries.

Samuel became converted, as did many of the people in his town. The community became a small, remote outpost of Zion.

Missionaries were few in those days. When the missionaries left Samuel's remote town, there was little communication with the Church till missionaries came again, several years later. Meanwhile, the people of the town built a church. They built a school so the next generation could learn to read and write. They maintained a well-organized Sunday School. Instead of drifting from lack of constant Church communication, the town stayed true to gospel principles. Eighty-five percent of the community became members of the Church. Samuel was eventually made branch president, in which calling he served for many years.

One of the occasional missionaries to visit the area was a young man named George Albert Smith. He was on a train when they passed the community. To start up a gospel conversation he tapped the man in front of him, pointed out the window and asked the man if he knew who those people were. "They are the Catawbas," the man answered.

"Do you know where they come from?" asked George Albert.

The man replied that they were Indians, and he didn't know where Indians came from.

George Albert explained to the man that those people were members of the House of Israel. A gospel discussion ensued.

Now, many years later, in April conference, 1950, President George Albert Smith recognized Chief Samuel Taylor Blue, chief of the Catawba tribe, and had him speak.

A year after Chief Samuel Blue's talk in the Tabernacle, he died at the age of eighty-five.

Chief Blue's legacy lives on in his descendants and descendants of the Catawba people who are still active today.

Musical Identity

P apers, passports, licenses, visas, photographs, permits, records—all manner of identification documents are part of our world in this century. Documents proclaim membership, citizenship and entitlements. Never is identification more important than in countries at war where correct identification is a matter of eating or starving, staying or moving, living or dying.

In the late 1930s, Denmark was a peaceful, prosperous, civilized country. Adhering to a policy of neutrality, Denmark was forced in 1939 to sign a peace treaty with Hitler's government. In 1940, violating their own treaty, the tanks of the Hitler's Third Reich rolled into the streets of neutral Denmark. The systematic confiscation of homes and properties began. The round up of "resisting" citizens and persons of "non-desirable" groups began. Danish law was suspended, martial law put in place. Executions, Gestapo terror, and deportments to concentration camps became a part of Danish life. Rationing, forced-labor, suspension of free speech, rewards for turning in fellow citizens, all the consequences of enemy invasion, caused many of the Danes to be filled with suspicion, fear, anger and desperation.

In Germany many Germans were experiencing the same circumstances and emotions. President Karl Herbert Klopfer of the East German Mission was drafted into the German army and sent to the battlefield. From a distance he struggled to direct the affairs of the Church in his area. The mission home in Berlin was destroyed and families were evacuated.

In 1943, Brother Klopfer, age thirty-two, was stationed near Esbjerg in Denmark, far from home. On a Sunday before Christmas, as he walked the streets of Esbjerg, he felt the need to worship, but it did not seem possible. He was dressed in full military uniform, in a country that despised him, while serving a government that would punish him if he did meet with a foreign church group. Still, he felt the need to worship. He did not know if there was a branch of the Church in Esbjerg. He wondered how he could possibly identify himself to them even if he found the Church. Then he thought of one way of identifying himself. As he walked the streets, he hummed the tune of a favorite Mormon hymn.

Finally, a little girl, skipping along the sidewalk on her way to church, stopped and asked in Danish, "Mormon?"

Brother Klopfer nodded his head. The little girl took the enemy soldier by the hand and led him to the meeting house.

When the branch president and members of the congregation saw the enemy soldier at the back entrance of the meeting place, there was concern. They wondered if this enemy soldier had come to hurt them. The branch president went to the back of the meeting house. Brother Klopfer did not speak Danish and the German language was not appreciated, so communication was made in English. Brother Klopfer identified himself and his desire to worship with the Saints. The branch president asked Brother Klopfer if he would be willing to take off his weapon belt in order to worship with them. Brother Klopfer removed it, knowing that a uniformed soldier removing his weapon belt and worshiping with a group in enemy country, if discovered, could be punished by death.

The branch president asked Brother Klopfer if he would deliver a gospel sermon at this Christmas time. Brother Klopfer spoke in English while Brother William Orum Pederson translated. He told about his own circumstances and bore testimony of the gospel.

Brother Klopfer's talk transcended national identities. In that meeting place they were all members of a higher kingdom, the kingdom of God. Brother Klopfer's passport to that meetingplace had not been a piece of paper, but a Mormon hymn.

Brother Klopfer did not survive the war. He died in a Russian prisoner-of-war camp. But the Danish Saints recorded the story of the man led to a sacrament meeting by a Mormon hymn.

His story was not his only legacy, however. If you open the L.D.S. hymnal to hymn number 298, you will see the name of Klopfer. Brother Klopfer's son, W. Herbert Klopfer, a member of the General Church Music Committee, and his family, carry on that legacy today—the love for, and unifying power of the hymns of the restored gospel of Jesus Christ.

Hero for Peace

T he man brought his bags to airport security. As was cus-
tomary in an iron-curtain country, the bags were searched.
The inspector found banned books. They were Books of
Mormon. A person faced imprisonment for trying to smuggle banned
objects into the country. The inspector looked at the illegal books,
looked at the man, then waved him through, banned books and all.

The man had refused to join the Communist party in his iron cur-
tain country. He traveled abroad, and when he returned to his country and stated that he had joined The Church of Jesus Christ of Latter-
day Saints, he was widely condemned. One newspaper proclaimed,

> There is no single forum in the city which, upon hearing of (his)
> activities, has not condemned him and asked that he be prevented
> from continuing.
>
> The meeting of the Socialist Alliance of Vostarnica II was even
> sharper in condemning such activity . . . the members of this city
> commune posed the question of possible pressures which may have
> induced this young man to accept an ideology which is completely
> alien to the ideals of our youth . . . .
>
> Veterans organizations of the city of Zadar have demanded a
> speedy and clear-cut solution of (his) religious activity. "Veterans
> condemn the activity of this popular sportsman," president [of the
> veterans organization] Rudi Basic stated. "We have requested that
> the communal committee consider this case." . . . The president of
> the League of Communists organization in *Vostarnica I* stated that
> his organization will fight against the intention of (him) to misuse
> his apartment for religious rites.

Thus went the criticism. Yet the young man survived and continued to worship in his apartment and invite others to worship with

him. In spite of the threats, the young man was unmolested. He was a powerful man in his country, not because he was a politician or party member, but because he was a national hero. And he was a national hero because he could play basketball. As a member of the Yugoslavian Olympic basketball team, he won the silver medal in Mexico City. He was privileged to go to America for an education. He had a choice of colleges, but while bicycling through Utah, he chose BYU. There he learned of the gospel and joined the Church.

As his basketball career continued, he became the first non-American to win All-American honors. He received those honors for two years, 1972 and 1973. Representing his country of Yugoslavia, he won a bronze Olympic Medal in 1972, a silver medal in 1976, and a gold medal in 1980. He became the only Mormon Olympian to have a set of bronze, silver, and gold medals. Rejecting a professional basketball career in the United States, he returned to Yugoslavia to coach the national team and to oversee the infancy of the Church in that part of the world.

Watching the ever-brewing turmoil between ethnic factions in his country, the man predicted the civil war that would tear his country apart long before it happened. He coached basketball in Greece and continued to help with the Church in that area of the world.

When civil war broke out in the former Yugoslavia, he did not turn his back in favor of a comfortable professional career far from the strife. He went back to his country and volunteered to work for peace. Because he was a hero in his country, he could go back and forth between the warring parties. He witnessed the tremendous suffering of his countrymen on both sides. He compared it to scenes from the Book of Mormon.

In 1992, he was appointed Croatia's deputy ambassador to the United States. In 1994, he was named Croatia's acting ambassador to the United States.

In May of 1995, at the age of forty-six, he died of cancer. In 1996, he was elected to the Basketball Hall of Fame in Springfield, Massachusetts. He was a hero in the sport of basketball, a hero to his country, and a hero in the gospel—Kresimir Cosic.

Super Star

The Church of Jesus Christ of Latter-day Saints has always been an active supporter of the arts. From the beginning of the Church, Mormon communities have boasted bands, choirs, artwork, theaters. Coming west to Utah, the hardships of the trek were lightened by music and dance. Brigham Young quipped, "Tight laced religious professors of the present generation have a horror at the sound of a fiddle. There is no music in hell, for all good music belongs to heaven."

Artemus Ward, in his travels to Utah, recorded, "The Mormons are fond of dancing. Brigham and Heber C. dance . . . The Prophet is more industrious than graceful as a dancer. He exhibits, however, a spryness of legs quite remarkable in a man of his time of life. I didn't see Heber C. Kimball on the floor. I am told he is a loose and reckless dancer, and that many a lily-white toe has felt the crushing weight of his cowhide monitors." He recorded also, "Brigham Young says the devil has monopolized the good music long enough, and it is high time the Lord had a portion of it . . . The Mormons, by the way, are preeminently an amusement loving people, and the Elders pray for the success of their theater with as much earnestness as they pray for anything else . . . The congregation (at the theater) doesn't startle us. There are no ravishingly beautiful women present, and no positively ugly ones. The men are fair to middling. They will never be slain in cold blood for their beauty, nor shut up in jail for their homeliness."

When first arriving in the Salt Lake Valley, the Saints built a roofed, open-walled meeting place they called "The Old Bowery." By 1851, theatricals were being staged there. In 1852, the "Social Hall" was completed and used for dances, receptions and theatricals.

In 1862, before the temple was finished or before there was a capitol building, The Salt Lake Theatre was completed. It was spacious and elegant, seating fifteen hundred people and decorated with the finest ornaments that Mormon artists could provide. It was the first theater west of the Mississippi. The ornate theater in the midst of the pioneer West demonstrated the unlikely combination of the refined and the rustic, the sophisticated and the countrified. Because of the poverty of the Saints, tickets were purchased with whatever they had. One man paid with a large turkey and received two chickens as change. Orson F. Whitney recorded, "We went early to the Theatre in those days. The doors opened at 6:30 p.m., and performances began at seven. During the waits between acts, lively domestic conversation often went on in the usually crowded auditorium. One evening, just as the orchestra had suddenly finished a fine overture with a mighty crash, a woman's voice shrilled out upon the silence: 'We fry ours in butter!' At another time a good sister with a new set of false teeth—the first that ever crossed the plains—took them out of her mouth and passed them along the row where she was sitting, that all might have a close-up view of the 'grinding monopoly.'"

Nationally-known actors traveled to Salt Lake City to perform in the lushly appointed facility. International celebrities, such as Oscar Wilde, lectured there. Mostly it was local actors who displayed their talents in the Salt Lake Theater. One of the local actresses, who developed her skills on that stage and then moved on to perform in other theaters across the country, was named Annie. Her parents joined the Church as it was moving west. Annie was born in 1848, three weeks after her parents arrived in the Great Salt Lake Valley. She got her first acting role at the Social Hall in 1856, when she was eight-years-old. After the Salt Lake Theatre was built, she won roles on its stage. She became one of the leading actresses in the Deseret Dramatic Company. Once, she attracted the attention of an out-of-towner named James Kiskadden. He was not a member of the Church. He came night after night to the theater to see Annie perform the same role. He would not miss her performances. In 1869, Annie and James were married. The union produced one living child whom they named Maude.

One of the great veteran actors of the Salt Lake Theatre was Phil Margetts. For years he was a leading actor in Utah. (Decades later a theater would be named for him at Brigham Young University.) At one time, Margetts appeared in a farce called *The Lost Child*. He was to play the panicky father of a lost baby. Instead of getting a real baby for the play, the prop man came up with a grotesque looking rag doll. Margetts fumed. He would not go on stage with that sorry excuse for a baby. The prop man stammered his explanation: The rag doll was the best he could do on short notice. He couldn't get a live baby. Nobody would lend him one.

"What!" exclaimed Margetts, "In Utah! Where babies are our best crop!"

A volunteer live baby was found. But a great deal of distress ensued backstage when the baby would not stop fussing and wailing. Phil refused to go on. The situation was saved when Annie Kiskadden snatched up her baby, little Maude, from her cradle and offered her for the part. The show went on and Margetts played his part with a tenderness and sincerity that could never have been evoked by the rag doll. That was little Maude Kiskadden's first role upon the stage.

Shortly after Maude's debut, Annie and James Kiskadden moved to San Francisco. In the family's travels following the acting profession, Maude grew up performing. She used the name of Maude Adams (her mother's maiden name) upon the stage. Maude became one of the most noted and celebrated actresses of the American stage. She met a Scottish playwright named James Barrie. He was so impressed with her that he wrote plays for her. One of the plays he wrote, with her in mind for the leading role, was *Peter Pan*. Though Maude was not in the London debut of that play, she played the role in New York for years.

Maude was a super star for her era. In spite of her celebrated status, Maude remembered her Utah ties. In 1911, she hosted the Tabernacle Choir on their tour to New York, treating them to a performance and a backstage reception. She spent much of her time doing charity work for orphans and entertaining the troops during World War I. She never married, preferring solitude when she was not on the stage or involved in charitable causes. This only added to the mystery of the woman. After the war, her health broken, she retired, leaving the world of the theater. Maude Adams, the super star of her age, disappeared from public view. In 1953, at the age of eighty-two, Maude Adams died, her death almost unnoticed by the world.

But there is more to the story of Maude Adams. In the 1970s, a writer named Richard Matheson was touring a museum in Virginia City, Nevada. On the wall of the museum hung the picture of a beautiful woman, an actress who had once played in Virginia City. Matheson was captivated by the photograph. He had to find out who the woman was. He researched her story. He wrote a novel, *Bid Time Return*, suggested by the picture he had seen of Maude Adams. The novel was made into a movie, *Somewhere in Time*, starring Jane Seymore and Christopher Reeve. For a while Maude Adams, the super star of another era, was remembered once again.

The Mysterious Substance

Pioneers in early Utah didn't know what it was. They'd never seen anything like it. Veins of the black substance were found in areas of what are now Uintah and Duchesne counties.

The black stuff with a high luster looked like coal, but it didn't work like coal. It crumbled in your hands, turning to powder. There didn't seem to be a single use for it.

An adventurer named Sam Gilson lived among the Mormons, though he was not a Mormon himself. Sam was a rider for the Pony Express. He served as an Indian scout and interpreter. In 1853 he was at the ceremony celebrating the laying of the cornerstone of the Salt Lake Temple. He was also at Promontory, Utah, on May 10, 1869, to witness the driving of the golden spike that linked the first Transcontinental railroad.

While associating with Indians in the Uintah region, Sam Gilson noticed them using a substance that looked like coal, but that crumbled in your hand. The Indians were using it to waterproof baskets. Sam Gilson found veins of the substance. He staked claims and sold the stuff to companies to waterproof barrels. That was the beginning of the "Gilsonite" industry. More uses were discovered. At first it was mined by hand and transported by wagon. In 1957, a refinery was built in Gilsonite, Colorado, across the border from Utah, to process the substance. Today, Gilsonite is used mainly to produce coke for use in the aluminum industry. It is the first raw material other than crude oil that can produce conventional petroleum products. It is also used in the manufacture of asphalt floor tiles, brake linings, electrical insulation, paints, battery boxes, printing inks, waterproofing and insulating high-temperature piping. Over the years the substance provided employment for many people in the area.

There was a reason the pioneers didn't know what the substance was. There was a reason the pioneers had never seen it before. Except for tiny traces elsewhere, the Utah area is the only place in the world where Gilsonite is found.

Playing with Guns

Two of the original buildings from the Mormon era still standing in Nauvoo, Illinois, are the Jonathan Browning home and gun shop. The restored site is where Jonathan Browning invented several types of repeating rifles.

When the Saints were driven from Nauvoo, the main body of the Church moved west to Utah. Jonathan stayed in Iowa for several years to help outfit the pioneers going west. Finally emigrating to Utah himself, Jonathan and his family moved to Ogden where he reestablished his business. His sons, especially John Moses and Matthew, showed aptitude for the family business from childhood. When John Moses was ten years old, he built a gun from scrap parts he found on the trash heap. It was a makeshift affair. He went hunting with his brother Matthew. When the gun was fired, one sage hen was dead, two sage hens were senseless, and John Moses was knocked down. The two boys thought they would catch heck from their father for playing with guns. Jonathan, however, after eating sage hen pie, looked over John Moses' gun and said, "John Moses, you're going on eleven. Can't you make a better gun than that?"

John Moses did go on to invent better guns. He got his first patent in 1879 when he was just twenty-four. One hundred and twenty-seven more patents would follow during his lifetime.

In 1885, the Winchester Repeating Arms Company was impressed by the simple and effective design of John's and Matthew's breech-loading single-shot rifle. They bought the patent and are still producing the gun today. Winchester bought the patents for forty-three more of John's inventions.

Though he took time off to serve a mission for the LDS Church, John was soon back with his inventions. Other companies besides Winchester purchased John's inventions as well—Colt, Remington,

Stevens and others. The 1890 Colt machine gun, nicknamed the "Peacemaker," was adopted by the U.S. Army and first used in the Spanish-American War. In 1896, a Browning automatic pistol came into use by the U.S. Army. The Browning Automatic Rifle, designed in 1917, was the standard automatic weapon the U.S. Army used until the Korean War.

Quiet, unassuming and publicity-shy, John Moses Browning found himself acclaimed as one of the greatest inventors of small arms in history and foremost in the field of automatic weapons. Some credited him with enabling the Allies to win World War I. Over the course of four wars, millions have carried weapons of his design into battle. His portrait hangs in the Inventors Gallery of the Smithsonian Institution. King Albert of Belgium presented him with The Cross of Knighthood of the Order of Leopold. A memorial plaque in Liege, Belgium, acclaims John as the greatest firearm inventor in the history of the world.

John died of illness in Belgium in 1926 while working on another arms invention. His body was sent home to Ogden, Utah, where he is buried.

The modest genius gunsmith, who began as a child fiddling with guns, is recognized as the designer of the Remington auto-loading shotguns and rifles, Winchester repeating shotguns, Stevens rifles and Colt automatic pistols. His inventions are still in use today.

A Wild West Tale

Williiam was born in 1846. In 1857, his father died and the eleven-year-old became the family bread winner. He got a job helping drive the cattle and wagons taking supplies to Johnston's Army.

Johnston's Army was sent by President Buchanan to Utah to put down a rumored Mormon uprising. The decision to send the army to Utah, later called by historians "Buchanan's Blunder," was a serious one to the Saints. Brigham Young sent Lot Smith and his men to do whatever it took to stop the army so that communications could be opened with President Buchanan. Lot Smith was commanded to delay the army, but at the same time, not to take a human life. He achieved this by cutting off supplies to the army. Lot Smith and his men waylaid the supply train of Lewis Simpson, where young William worked.

The supply wagons were burned, except for one that held the possessions, supplies, even the arms, of the drivers, and enabled them to go back safely. Young William had been a part of this episode of the Wild West. He was witness to the war that claimed no lives in battle.

William found other work. Thrilling to the tales of Kit Carson, General Freemont, and others touted in the popular press of the day, he wanted to be just like them. William took work with the Pony Express, he scouted for the U.S. cavalry, he looked for gold. In 1868, William got a job hunting and shooting buffalo to furnish meat for the Kansas Pacific railway. He was so good at his job, so sure a shot with his gun, that the railroad workers gave him the nickname of "Buffalo Bill."

Buffalo Bill again scouted for the Army. His exploits were glorified in popular fiction. He realized the worth of publicity. He loved the celebrity of appearing in pulp novels. He acted in plays in New York. He acted in a show with his friend "Wild Bill" Hickok which depicted Mormons as villains. In 1883, Buffalo Bill started his "Wild West" exhibition. He traveled with his Wild West Show all over the East and across the ocean to Europe. He recreated Indian battles and touted such celebrities as Little Annie Oakley and Sitting Bull.

Buffalo Bill's heart belonged to the West. At the end of each show season he would return to the West, establishing a ranch in the Big Horn Basin and hunting in Utah. Times had changed and his differences with the Mormons had changed. What mattered by then was if his Mormon companions were good hunters. An 1893 expedition included Buffalo Bill, Major Milemey (who was Queen Victoria's personal guard), world-class crack-shot Johnny Baker, and Mormon leaders such as Edwin Dee Woolley and Junius Wells.

That was the way of the Wild West. Friends made enemies and enemies made friends. It didn't matter to Buffalo Bill Cody, as long as it made a good story.

Reverse Psychology

S peaking of his call to the Apostleship of The Church of Jesus Christ of Latter-day Saints, Brigham Young said, "Doubtless many of the Elders think that they are smarter than I am. As brother Kimball has said, some of the knowing ones marveled when we were called to the Apostleship. It was indeed a mystery to me; but when I consider what consummate blockheads they were, I did not deem it so great a wonder."

Brigham Young, second president of the Church, understood human frailty, including his own. He admitted from the pulpit, "It is much easier to stand up and talk for an hour than to sit and listen—for everyone knows that the mind can't conceive what the seat can't endure."

In running the Church, Brigham Young was practical and often brusque. Judge Daniel Harrington recorded the story of a man who had the impression that President Young had the gift of interpreting dreams. "This individual had been troubled with quite a fantastic dream throughout the night. So in the morning, he told of his exciting dream and asked President Young if he could give him an interpretation of it. The President listened to his statement. After the dreamer had finished, Brigham Young asked, 'What did you have for your supper last evening, Brother Jones?' The party answered, 'Well, I had quite a hearty dinner. I had some pork chops, some vegetables, and I ate half a mince pie for dessert.' The President looked at him in a quizzical way, and said, 'Brother Jones, you go home tonight and eat the other half of that mince pie and you'll get the interpretation.'"

One woman came to Brigham sobbing. "My husband keeps telling me to go to hell," she cried.

Brigham patted her kindly and advised, "Don't go."

Another time Brigham used reverse psychology to get someone to stay active in the Church. As J. Golden Kimball told it, "I remember hearing about a saying of President Young to a brother who was terribly tried. His case came before the High Council, and the council had decided against the man. You know it happens sometimes, when the decision is not in your favor, you feel disgruntled. And some leave the Church because of the actions of men; they feel they have been dealt with unjustly. Brother Brigham, on the occasion referred to, said to the brother in sarcasm, 'Now apostatize and go to hell.' And the brother ejaculated, 'I won't do it; this is just as much my church as it is yours, and I am going to stay with it.'"

To spite Brother Brigham, the man stayed active in the Church.

A New Trend

They had them in ancient Rome. They had them in the bazaars of Istanbul. But the idea was something new and original in the United States. In a country conditioned to independent shops, department stores and "Main Street America," the idea was risky. Critics said it wouldn't work here. Critics said people wouldn't come. Critics said Americans wouldn't give up their "Main Street."

Sidney Horman had a different idea. In a country which after World War II was increasingly suburban, he thought the time was ripe. He thought that if you took a bunch of smaller stores, put them together, located them away from downtown, then put a roof over the whole project, people would go there to shop.

In 1954, Sid built the first one in Las Vegas. It worked. He tried later in Holladay, Utah. The idea swept the nation. Today, the idea is a standard part of American life.

That is how Mormon builder and contractor Sidney M. Horman came up with the first covered "shopping mall" in the United States.

Healing Stones

D avid killed Goliath with a stone. An ancient punishment was death by stoning. But sometimes rocks can heal.

In the early settlement of the Utah Territory, Brigham Young called some pioneer families to go settle a distant and desolate place on the Muddy River. One pioneer family called to settle "The Muddy" started south over the mountains. In this family was a six-year-old girl named Sarah. Sarah owned a singularly ugly doll. Her older brother had carved a crude head on a pine limb. Mother had stained the face with blue and red dye and wrapped it in colorful scraps of cloth to make it cuddly. To most people it would have seemed a hideous toy, but to a little girl who had never seen a store-bought doll, she was beautiful. Sarah cherished her doll.

One day, while camped in a rugged, mountainous area, native Indian women from a nearby camp came to visit the family. Brigham Young had instructed the settlers to get along with the migratory Indian tribes at all costs. He advised the settlers to share what they had with them. One of the Indian women saw Sarah's peculiar doll.

There is an identity among cultures about dolls. Every culture seems to know what a doll is for. The Indian woman was charmed by the doll's little brown face and colored clothes. She indicated to the pioneer family that she wanted the doll. Sarah was crushed when Mother calmly explained to her that she would have to make the sacrifice of her most prized possession. Mother told Sarah to be brave and loving till Sarah, restraining sobs, was able to go to the Indian woman and place her beloved dolly in the woman's arms. The Indian woman then presented the doll to the little Indian girl by her side. Six-year-old Sarah went back to the wagon where she climbed in, wrapped herself in the quilts, and cried.

Nobody is sure why the accident happened. Some time had passed when Sarah came out of the wagon and, missing the wagon tongue, she fell, striking her face on the hard wood. Blood gushed from her nose. Mother picked her up and carried her to the nearby stream where she bathed her face in the cold water.

Time passed and the loss of blood would not stop. Sarah became pale and weak. The family was frightened as Sarah's condition grew serious. They thought it must be a hemorrhage from a broken blood vessel and they didn't know what to do.

In a panic Mother realized she was in the mountains, far from other settlements, far from any help. Then suddenly she remembered, there was somebody nearby. Mother ran to the Indian camp. She indicated as best she could that she needed help. Three Indian women came back with her. When they saw Sarah they immediately went to work. At the stream, they made a bed of flat stones and laid Sarah there. Then they put small, smooth pebbles on Sarah's neck, her face and across her nose. Every few minutes they replaced the pebbles with others from the stream. They kept this up until the flow of blood stopped. Though Sarah was weak, there was confidence that she was out of danger. She was put to bed in the wagon. The Indian women stayed with Sarah all day to make sure she was out of danger.

Today it may seem that a life can not be saved by putting rocks on the face—that is, unless we understand something important. The small, smooth pebbles that were placed on Sarah's neck, face and nose were selected from the nearby stream—a stream that was frigid from mountain runoff. As the stones warmed, they were replaced by other cold ones. The Indian women were applying a primitive form of what we now call a "cold pack." This slowed the blood flow to Sarah's face, allowing it time to coagulate. A little girl's life was saved by stones.

One of the last things that Sarah remembered that night was being tucked into her quilts by an Indian woman who patted her, spoke to her and placed in her arms an ugly, much loved, wooden doll.

The Red Ghost

The most bizarre monsters to haunt the American West lived in the second half of the nineteenth century. Many a lonely traveler or prospector, sitting around his campfire at night, was frightened by the sight of a ten-foot tall, hairy beast with dreadfully deformed face, staring at him from the darkness. Indians, watching their horses and cattle skitter and stampede, knew when the alien monsters were near.

In 1846, the U.S. Army's Mormon Battalion trekked across the American Southwest to Texas and across to California. The worst creatures they encountered then were wild Texas bulls. After the Mormons came to the Salt Lake Valley, they began to spread out, creating settlements throughout the Utah territory, which at that time included much of Nevada and Arizona. By the 1860's, there were several Mormon settlements in what would become Arizona. It was in Arizona that the most bizarre accounts of the monsters were reported.

As horrible as the monsters were, there was one that was worse than them all. It was called the "Red Ghost." It was not only large and hairy, but it had a red tint to its hair and a terrible stench. It terrorized the settlements. There was one unsubstantiated report that it killed a person. The most horrifying feature of the beast was the horrible thing on its back, a gruesome rider. Not till it was purportedly shot and killed did the reign of the Red Ghost end. The other monsters continued to be seen, occasionally, till just after the turn of the century, when it was thought the last ones were killed either by Indians or mule skinners.

How the monsters got to the West in the first place is another story. In the mid-1800s, the American West was mostly uncharted wilderness. Persons of influence in Washington, D.C., considered how best to transport supplies and people over the vast stretches of desolate terrain. Mules, horses, oxen—all had their drawbacks. But there was one creature that might be able to conquer the West. It was big and it was hairy. It could carry 800 pounds. It could travel thirty-five to seventy-five miles a day, twice what a mule team could. It needed no shoes on its feet. It would eat the desert bushes that mules and horses refused. And it needed water only at long intervals. It was decided. The government would bring camels to the United States.

In 1856, with the approval of the Secretary of War, the first camels arrived from the Middle East. They were one-humped dromedaries, standing about six feet high at the shoulders, with long necks that could loom even higher. Lieutenant Edward F. Beale, with a train of seventy-seven camels and their babies, mapped wagon roads through what is now Arizona. Though Beale and several others firmly believed in the camels, mule-skinners, packers and teamsters hated them. The camels spooked the horses and cattle. And they were . . . unnatural. Beale challenged six of his camels against twelve of the packer's mules with their wagons. The challenge was a sixty-mile trek with equal loads. The camels did it in two-and-a-half days. The mules took four days. The camels foraged on local vegetation. The mules needed to be fed.

Meanwhile, in Washington, D.C., President James Buchanan and his war cabinet considered using camels against the supposed Mormon rebellion in 1857. Johnston's army was coming from the east, and an army of camels from the west might cut off any retreat. Those camel plans were dropped when the army got to Utah and couldn't find a rebellion to fight.

As for Lieutenant Beale, his command of the camel caravan was short-lived. The Civil War came and officers were recalled. The camel project was disbanded. Some of the camels were set free. Most were auctioned off to transporters and miners for hauling freight, water and ore. Some of these were later set free by those who could not manage them.

On the opposite side of the Great Basin, mining barons of the Comstock camps imported Bactrian camels from Mongolia to help with the mining. The Bactrian camels had two humps and were considered even stranger. Normally docile animals, the camels became vicious from overwork and abuse. Ill treatment caused them to spit, kick, and bite their human handlers.

One of the lead camels of the Comstock was a bad-tempered beast named "Old Brigham." The press in Salt Lake City had decried the gambling, drunkenness and other vices of the mining camps. In retaliation for that criticism, miners had named the old camel after the Mormon leader. The camel lived up to his tough reputation. He was known to chase a man over a mile if the man tried to harass him. Many a citizen had a laugh at some fool cowboy being pursued down the street by a livid camel.

The camels spooked horses and cattle. Teamsters complained. There was an unwillingness on the part of miners to tolerate the camels' bad temper. Eventually the Comstock camels were let loose to forage and travel wherever they would. They were spotted by travelers for years afterward.

Legend has it that in Colorado, drunken miners got hold of one of the Arizona dromedaries. It was a big brute with rusty-red colored hair. One of the miners' comrades had died, so they used leather straps to tie the corpse on the camel's back. The camel was then set loose. Driven mad by the stench of the corpse, the camel terrorized northern Arizona, losing grisly bits of the corpse along the way. When the Red Ghost was finally killed, only the leather straps were left.

How much of the story is fact, and how much is elaboration, no one really knows. The Red Ghost has entered the realm of legend. But one thing is sure. More than one early settler was scared into rapid repentance by the sight of a "monster" the likes of which he'd never seen before.

The Man Who Got Coal for Christmas

Christmas was a special time in the home of George and Lucy. There was a fresh, pine Christmas tree with candles. The home smelled of mince pies, spicy doughnuts and plum pudding. Most of the holiday foods were packed on a sled and dragged over the snow to the ward house. It was thrilling for the children to help their parents deliver the gifts to their ward for distribution to those who are overlooked at Christmas time.

Money was carefully budgeted for family gifts. Each child hung a stocking on the fireplace on Christmas Eve. But for father, George, it was never enough. He insisted that Santa could never get all the things he wanted into a regular sock. He had a huge sock for the occasion. And to insure that he got the most presents, he set his two tall rubber boots by the fireplace as well. Delicious mince pie and milk were set out for Santa to thank him for his generosity.

Alas, George's plan did not work. On Christmas morning the children found their stockings stuffed with goodies and gifts. But George's huge sock and his tall boots were stuffed with coal, sticks and vegetables.

The children laughed, then feeling sorry for their daddy, shared their own.

In the afternoon George took the children with him as he visited those less fortunate with tokens of remembrance. Though George and his family were not rich, his children saw true poverty as they brought holiday cheer to those in need.

One year George fell seriously ill. Expenses were high and George could not work. There was no money for the traditional turkey dinner or Christmas treats or gifts for themselves, let alone for others. There was no money for even the smallest stocking. There was no money for Christmas—unless they took the tithing money they had saved. While George lay ill, the decision rested on mother Lucy's shoulders. Would that money be for her family or for the Lord? Could she look at her childrens' faces and deny them any holiday comfort at this sad time? Lucy finally made her decision. It was the Lord's money and she had no right to it. Before she could be tempted more, she put on her wraps and hurried to the bishop where the tithing was paid in full.

Lucy walked in the snow toward home with her head down. Her heart was heavy. Then she heard a voice call out to her. It was a neighbor, Mark Austin. He said, "I have been thinking that your expenses have been exceedingly heavy during George's long illness, so I should like very much to have you take this little gift and buy yourself something very special for Christmas. I am sure you haven't had anything for yourself in a long, long time." Lucy, tears choking her, took the check with grateful heart and hurried home. At home she held the check before the lights and was amazed to see that the amount was the exact same as she had paid for tithing. She related the story to her family and that Christmas became known as the "Tithing Christmas."

George recovered and shared many more Christmases with his family—some plentiful and some meager—but always sharing Christmas with others.

George went on to become the eighth president of The Church of Jesus Christ of Latter-day Saints. George Albert Smith served for almost six years with Lucy by his side—the man who once got coal, sticks and vegetables in his boots for Christmas.

The Kid Who Drove Cars

H e drove around the county in a big Buick touring car. In a family trip to Wyoming on treacherous roads, he'd proved his mettle. And since his father was so busy, Bill became the official driver for the family. Almost daily he drove the Buick into the city. One day the police ran him in. The desk sergeant lectured him for fifteen minutes. He wasn't supposed to drive. You had to be sixteen there to operate a motor vehicle. At the time Bill was pulled in by the police, he was only fourteen.

Bill's run-in with the police had little effect on the boy. He continued to drive the Buick around town. The police got tired of running the boy in. Finally they just waved him on.

Bill was used to doing things other people thought a kid shouldn't or couldn't do. He'd been a cowboy from the time he could ride a horse. He rode the range and herded sheep. At age thirteen he tracked and killed two bears that were stalking the sheep herds. When his father was away or occupied, he ran the farm, tended the cows, organized the family and laborers, sold the crops and brought in profits.

Once, when he was fourteen, Bill was given the responsibility of herding between two thousand and three thousand sheep to the railroad yard, loading them into ten cars, riding with the train over a thousand miles from home to a place he'd never been before, selling the sheep and bringing home a profit.

The next year he took a load of sheep the other direction to Omaha. Halfway through the journey problems occurred. The conductor noticed that Bill was just a kid. The conductor said it was against Union Pacific rules for anyone under eighteen to ride with adults on the freight train. But the sheep needed constant tending along the way, so the railroad vowed to care for the sheep, and Bill was forced to take a passenger train to the destination. In Omaha Bill waited for the sheep but they never came. The railroad had lost the sheep. It took days of telephone calls, telegrams and interviews for Bill to undo the mistakes that the adults had made.

Bill also wanted to go on a mission for the LDS Church while he was quite young, but the Church wouldn't let him go until he was nineteen. The mission was a challenge, but Bill succeeded in spite of being shot at, chased by mobs, frozen in winter, and having doors constantly slammed in his face. His enthusiasm for the work did not die.

At the end of his two-year mission he stopped in Washington D.C. He wanted to see the sights. What he saw were crowds of tourists sweltering in the summer heat. He saw a pushcart peddler selling soda, ice cream, and lemonade who was sold out in minutes and had to go back to restock his cart to fill the needs of people. Bill got ideas.

From those first ideas and from the responsibility, tenacity, management skills and work ethic he'd learned as a kid, Bill founded an empire—a business empire that included restaurant chains, hotel chains, amusement parks, and feeding services that span the globe. The family empire prospered and lived on after his death in 1985.

Year after year, the Marriott family is recognized as one of the most successful in the country. The kid who drove cars later served as a director of American Motors Corporation. The kid who got hauled in by police for underage driving became an advisor to U.S. presidents. Such was the amazing story of J. Willard Marriott, Sr.

Tale of the Dead Coyote

Howard Egan was born in Ireland and emigrated to the United States where he joined the Church in 1842. During his lifetime he was a bodyguard to both Joseph Smith and Brigham Young. He served as an officer in the Nauvoo Legion, a militia organized jointly by Joseph Smith and the State Militia of Illinois. He came to Utah with the first Mormon wagon train. He served as a scout for the Mormon wagon trains and ran mail and communications between the Church and the U.S. Army's Mormon Battalion. He established routes to the West Coast for other wagon trains and selected the route for the U.S. mail line to California. Major Egan was a peacemaker with the Indians and managed a section of the Pony Express.

In the 1860's, in the rough expanse of western Utah Territory, Major Egan operated the Deep Creek Ranch. The ranch was part of the overland mail route. The complex served as a passenger station and supply station for those crossing the Great Basin to the West Coast. An office of the telegraph was also there, linking Salt Lake City with Carson City, Nevada. The Deep Creek Ranch was operated till 1869 when the transcontinental railroad made the way station unnecessary. During it's time of operation, however, the remote outpost had its share of adventures.

One evening at dusk, Major Egan was coming out of the stable when he saw a coyote enter the hen house. Major Egan ran quickly to the telegraph office where the shotgun was kept. "Ed," he called to the telegraph operator, "hand me the shotgun quick."

Ed asked what was the matter and Major Egan replied, "A coyote in the hen house!"

Instead of handing out the shotgun to Major Egan, Ed decided to handle the excitement himself. He came running with the gun to the hen house. "Where is the coyote?" he asked.

"Inside," said Egan. "Give me the gun and I will get him."

Ed wouldn't hand over the gun. It was dark in the hen house and nothing was clear, but Ed said, "I see him," and commenced shooting.

The commotion in the hen house was terrible for there were about a hundred chickens in addition to one scared coyote. Major Egan told Ed it was no use shooting into the hen house until they got a lantern so they could see the coyote. He had Ed stay were he was while he got the light.

When the light was brought, it was positioned so that they could see the coyote, upon which sight, Ed fired again. When the commotion and smoke died down, Major Egan dragged out the dead coyote as well as five or six large chickens that Ed had shot. Ed was proud of himself, but Major Egan was not happy about the loss of so many chickens. He was disgusted at Ed's enthusiastic shooting and thought about how to teach Ed a lesson.

Major Egan got up early the next morning. The coyote had frozen stiff during the night. Egan used sticks to prop up the stiff coyote in the garden, about thirty yards from the house. Then he hurried to the telegraph office, calling out for Ed to hand him the gun.

"What for?" Ed cried.

"A coyote in the garden," said Egan. "The gun, quick, before he goes."

Out came Ed with the gun saying, "Where is he?" Ed rushed around the corner of the house and said, "I see him—that's my hide." He quickly fired. The coyote squatted a bit.

"You missed him," said Egan.

Ed fired again. The coyote fell down. "I got him this time," Ed cried as he climbed over the fence and went to retrieve the kill so that he could place it next to the one he had bagged the night before. But when Ed grabbed it, the carcass was frozen stiff. He knew he had been tricked. He turned to accuse Major Egan, but Egan was nowhere to be seen. Egan was in the mess room telling the other men how Ed had just killed a dead coyote. There was merriment during breakfast at Ed's expense.

At dinner that evening, when all the men were seated around the table, the cook brought out the meal—cooked chicken. The men looked at Ed. Ed asked, "Is this the chickens the coyote killed?"

Answered the cook, "I guess so, for they were full of shot."

The Death Prophecy

P
resident Joseph F. Smith, sixth president of The Church of Jesus Christ of Latter-day Saints, once accompanied a friend to the hospital. The man's appendix had burst. Doctors consulted with each other. There seemed no hope. The burst appendix was surgically removed. Blood poisoning, so they said, in the third and last stage, had set in. Nine doctors were present. Of the nine, eight of the doctors said death for the patient was inevitable. Only one thought there was a chance the patient might pull through.

President Smith, on questioning the chief surgeon in the case, was told, "Mr. Smith, you need not think of such a possibility or probability as that this man shall live. Why, if he should live it would be a miracle, and this is not the day of miracles." The chief surgeon pronounced that the patient would die. Seven colleagues agreed. But one did not.

Miraculously, the patient recovered. But the pronouncement of the chief surgeon, the prophecy of impending death, was fulfilled—in a way—when the chief surgeon himself died. The patient lived.

While recovering, the patient sought out the doctor who, against the opinions of the others, believed the patient would survive. The patient asked the doctor why he had disagreed with his colleagues. The doctor explained that he had felt the pulse of thousands of patients in many hospitals, but he had never felt a pulse like this patient's. In all the tests he made on the patient during the hour and three-quarters that the surgery lasted, his heart had never missed one solitary beat. He made up his mind that heart would pull through.

That heart did pull through. The patient lived many more years and eventually he succeeded his friend President Joseph F. Smith in the leadership of the Church. He became the seventh President of The Church of Jesus Christ of Latter-day Saints—Heber J. Grant.

62

Put Them Right

J ohn lived in a rural area when he heard that some missionaries from a new church were going to hold a meeting in a schoolhouse. John was a cripple. He was in a wheelchair. There were great difficulties in getting John to the schoolhouse meeting. But John wanted to go. He had to go. He needed to hear those missionaries speak so that he could "put them right." He felt it was his responsibility to keep those missionaries in their place and make sure that no false doctrine was taught.

With the assistance of his strong sons, John was taken to the meeting in the schoolhouse and seated right down in front of the speakers. The missionaries told about the restoration of the gospel in these latter days, about the restoration of the priesthood, about the Book of Mormon. To the surprise of some, John did not interrupt the missionaries to dispute them. He did not "put them right." He listened.

When the meeting was over John asked his son to bring the missionaries to meet him. John invited the missionaries to spend the night at his home. The missionaries got little sleep however, for John kept them up till the wee hours of the morning discussing the gospel. Finally, John, noting his situation said, "If I weren't a cripple, I think I would like to apply for baptism."

One of the missionaries asked, "Do you think the Lord could heal you?"

"I think He could if He wanted to," answered John.

The missionaries read James 5:14, "Is any sick among you? Let him call for the elders of the church; and let them pray over him . . . ." After telling of the return of priesthood powers and the power of God to heal, the missionaries asked John if he would like them to administer to him. John answered that he would.

The missionaries administered to John. That next day John rose from his wheelchair and walked three-quarters of a mile to be baptized. He never went back to his wheelchair.

John and his family moved following the Church. He had many descendants, some of whom emigrated to Canada.

One of John's descendant's rose in the circles of political power. He became a legislator and speaker of the Alberta Legislature. He served as a minister in the Canadian government. He was a leader in Canadian industry, serving as president of Merrill Petroleums, director of the Toronto Dominion Bank of Canada, director of the National Trust Company, president of the Trans-Canada Pipe Line, president of the Canadian Gas Association, and many other influential positions. Finally, this descendant of John Tanner was appointed to his most important position—apostle, member of the Council of the Twelve, counselor to prophets David O. McKay, Joseph Fielding Smith, Harold B. Lee and Spencer W. Kimball.

John Tanner, the man who went to a schoolhouse to "put them right" was blessed with many great and worthy descendants including his great, great grandson—the legislator, apostle and counselor Nathan Eldon Tanner.

Half a World Away

When Robert, who grew up in Utah and California, received his mission call, he found himself called to an exotic location a hemisphere and an ocean away from home. He was called to serve in the far-off land of New Zealand among the Maori people.

Before leaving, Robert was given a blessing that he would have a knowledge of the language of the people amongst whom he would labor. He was sure of success in his labors. He was so confident that he didn't bother to study the language. When he got to New Zealand he couldn't speak the language. Three or four weeks passed and he still couldn't speak the language.

Finally, he had a dream that told him if he wanted the blessing, he had to work for it. After that, study time was set aside each day so that Robert could learn the language. The branch president where he was located also helped by assigning all the Primary children to help Robert to learn the language. The children taught Robert a song. He was proud to have learned an old Maori war chant till he learned that the translation of the Maori song was actually, "Hey diddle diddle, the cat and the fiddle, the cow jumped over the moon . . . ."

After a time Robert became fluent in the language of the Maoris and learned to love the people. Robert returned from his mission just as World War II broke out. All the missionaries serving in New Zealand were called home because of the war. President Matthew Cowley was left to run the New Zealand mission without official missionaries, so he used service men stationed in New Zealand to carry out the work when they were between military assignments.

Robert felt impressed that he was meant to continue his mission with the Maori people. He went into the air force and, sure enough, he was sent to San Francisco where all the Pacific processing was

done. He felt that he was going back to the Maori people and prepared himself for it. He was to ship out on a ship with several hundred men on their assignments to the Pacific.

About two days before the ship sailed, however, five men were
pulled from the Pacific assignment. Out of those hundreds of men,
five men were held back—including Robert. The five men were sent
all the way back across the U.S. to the East Coast for shipment across
the Atlantic, the opposite direction from where Robert felt he should
be. He consoled himself by thinking that perhaps he could work with
the Maoris again in the spirit world.

Robert was assigned to a convoy that crossed the Atlantic
Ocean. He saw the Rock of Gibralter go by. Finally his ship was
stopped in Egypt. In Cairo there was a small American air force
group. Of all the air force units in the world, this was one of the
smallest. And Cairo was about as far away from New Zealand as
anyone could hope to get. Robert had felt that he would do missionary work again among the Maoris. Instead, he'd ended up half a
world away from New Zealand. He said to himself, "Well, I don't
know what the Lord has in mind, but I'll just do the best I can, and
I am sure that everything will work out all right."

It took only a couple of days for Robert to understand. Of all
the places in the world, Cairo was the overseas processing base
for the entire Maori battalion. All the Maori soldiers were sent to
Cairo before being assigned to battle fronts in North Africa and
Italy. And the Maori base was stationed in the shadows of the
American air base.

For two years Robert worked in brotherhood with the Maoris,
worshiping with them, working with them, administering to them
and doing missionary work with them. The Maoris helped Robert
and Robert helped them—half a world away from their beloved
homeland.

During his military service, Robert was called to be the servicemen's coordinator for the Church in North Africa and the Middle

East. After the war, he returned to New Zealand, as president of the New Zealand Mission. Later, he became a chairman and director of several businesses and corporations. And later still he served in the Presiding Bishopric of the Church. As a member of the First Quorum of the Seventy, he obtained emeritus status in 1989—after a lifetime of service—Elder Robert L. Simpson.

The Cooperative Choir

In the late 1800's, as the population of the Utah Territory grew, several religious denominations established themselves in the sprouting communities. Members of the Roman Catholic faith depended on traveling priests for occasional ministrations. It is thought that Bonaventure Keller of Philadelphia offered the first known mass in Utah in July, 1859 at Camp Floyd.

In 1866, the Reverend Edward Kelly journeyed to Salt Lake City from California, rounded up the few Catholics in the city and celebrated Mass. He had no place to meet so President Brigham Young granted him use of the Assembly Hall on Temple Square.

Between 1868 and 1870, the Reverend James P. Foley came to Salt Lake City as the first resident pastor. The Catholics were still small in number. Foley met with three Catholic families in a home where a room was set aside as a temporary chapel. He found fourteen Catholic soldiers at Fort Douglas and held services for them. He soon obtained a small adobe structure for worship. Other traveling priests after Foley were again allowed to worship in the Mormon Assembly Hall where they sang High Mass. A brick church was finally built in 1871.

Then, in 1873, Father Lawrence Scanlan was assigned permanently to the territory. There were probably less than eight hundred Catholics in the territory at the time, and they were spread throughout the far-flung mining and railroad communities. Father Scanlan found ninety of them between Salt Lake City and Ogden. On Christmas Eve in 1874, the first Midnight Mass was celebrated in Utah. Father Scanlan traveled through the territory, organizing congregations and beginning construction of churches, schools and hospitals.

In 1879, Father Scanlan organized the building of a church and hospital in Silver Reef, a mining community in southern Utah near St. George. An affable man who had a knack of generating good will, Father Scanlan became familiar with many of the LDS leaders in the territory. While in southern Utah he had complained that since his church in Silver Reef was not finished, he had nowhere to perform High Mass for the local Catholics. In a short time an invitation came from Erastus Snow and other Mormon authorities. Father Scanlan was invited to hold Catholic services in the Mormon's St. George Tabernacle.

Father Scanlan accepted the invitation gladly but regretted that there was no choir to perform the music portion of the services. The St. George Tabernacle Choir, under the direction of Brother John Macfarlane, was volunteered. But the music for the mass was in Latin, which the choir members did not know, so Brother Macfarlane and the choir trained for six weeks learning the Latin mass. As the Catholics were still in the minority, there were not many to fill the congregation, so local LDS members filled the bulk of the congregation as well. On May 25, 1879, the first High Mass to be sung by a full, organized choir in Utah, was sung in the St. George Tabernacle by Mormons, in Latin.

Father Scanlan later became the first bishop of the Catholic Diocese of Salt Lake City.

A Modern Woman

Lula was a modern woman. Born to an LDS family she was naturally educated. Her love for learning caused her to ever seek for more enlightenment. She read constantly, and she wrote. She loved writing. In her youth she wrote articles, stories and poems. Some were published.

Like a modern woman, Lula debated in her mind and heart the difficulties in reconciling family and career. Like a modern woman, she wondered if it was possible to have both a family and a career and do justice to both callings. She wondered if it was possible to "have it all."

Lula wrote letters to an aunt for advice. Her aunt was a published and well-read poet, seemingly successful in both family and career responsibilities. Lula respected her aunt's perspectives. Lula's aunt wrote back that although giving birth was a prime purpose of womanhood, cultivating the minds of those already born was just as important. It was essential that those already born should be helped to be useful people.

Lula, when she was barely twenty-two years old, was a recognized author and was amazingly—for her youth—offered the editorship of a newspaper. She accepted. She was involved in her career, yet she wondered if that was the right thing. She wondered if it would be better for her to get married and have babies. Her aunt regretted that many women physically able to bear babies were incapable of adequately rearing and inspiring those children. Someone else must fill that role.

Life changed for Lula when, at the age of twenty-four, an incident occurred. She associated with a group of young people who went to dances and social events. Some young men had seemed interested in her. Some tried, unsuccessfully, to kiss her. One night after a dance, a bashful young man named Levi Richards asked if he could see her home. When they got to her place, he proposed marriage to her. Lula was surprised because she had no inkling that he liked her. She said she would pray about the matter. She did. She couldn't think of a reason not to marry Levi—he was of good character and she felt she could come to love him. In a short time they were married.

The children began to arrive, and Lula wrestled with the age-old questions of career and family. She experienced some health problems. Finally, after five years with the newspaper Lula asked to be released from her job as editor. She gave up her job, but she did not give up her career. She only changed direction. As she wrote in her farewell to readers, "I do not feel that I am bidding . . . 'a long and sad farewell' but hope, as a contributor, to still communicate . . . I have . . . decided that during the years of my life which may be properly devoted to the rearing of a family I will give my special attention to that most important branch of 'Home Industry.' Not that my interest in the public weal is diminishing, or that I think the best season of a woman's life should be completely absorbed in her domestic duties. But every reflecting mother, and every true philanthropist can see the happy medium between being selfishly home bound, and foolishly public spirited."

Lula continued to write as she reared her family. She contributed articles, essays and poems to various publications and eventually finished a book. She carried a notebook in her purse so she could write at any time. Her children remember how sometimes, during an evening meal, for instance, an idea would come to her and she would simply leave what she was doing to write. Dishes would be left unwashed, the house would be left uncleaned. The children would be left to dress themselves for bed. Still, she instilled in her children the love for learning and the written word. She bore seven children. Of the four children who lived to adulthood, one became a painter, one a colonizer, one a dentist, and one a professor of English.

Lula died at age ninety-five leaving two legacies. One legacy was her family. The other legacy was her achievements. Lula Greene Richards was Utah's first professional woman journalist. She had overseen, with the help of others, such as her aunt Eliza R. Snow, the birth of one of the influential newspapers of its time, the *Woman's Exponent*—the first continuous newspaper published by and for women west of the Mississippi. For the five years she served as editor she addressed women's rights, home health care, education and rearing of children, advice to young women, and women's suffrage. The bimonthly newspaper/journal was read by thousands of women in the U.S. and Great Britain. The influential paper which Lula Greene Richards had helped to birth was published for forty-two years.

As a young woman, still living at home, Lula had written this poem which expressed her feelings at the time, and which came to express her life:

> Did I stay too long in the schoolroom
> After lessons were through
> Leaving my mother and sisters
> With all my work to do? . . .
>
> Forgive me, my mother and sisters,
> Smile kindly and gently speak;
> I'll try to do better tomorrow
> And all the rest of the week. . .
>
> For I have been writing something
> Which will likely be read
> By our children's children
> After we all are dead;
> And must I think I should have been
> Washing dishes instead?

The Runaway

Matt was a mischievous boy. At two-and-a-half-years-old he ran away from home. After a frantic search involving the police he was found almost two miles from home with another two-year-old he had taken with him. Fun-loving, though never cruel, he found ways to keep things stirred up.

One winter's day when snow was piled high, Matt created an ice slick in front of his house, then stood nearby to direct passers-by safely around it, hoping they would tip him for his kindness. All he earned was a nickel and a warning.

He made jokes in Sunday School. He brought snakes, frogs and toads to school and let them loose in the classroom—though he would always own up in a way that made even the teacher laugh. On one occasion he took a newspaper from a neighbor's doorstep. He divided the newspaper into two sections, and sold the two sections as two separate newspapers.

The pranks ran both ways. Some of the men in his ward used to get him to sit in a ditch for a nickel. They ended up owing him thirty cents.

As a child, Matt was expected to join in family prayers. He thought his father one of longest prayers in the world. His father used prayers not only for thanks and supplication, but to bear his testimony and to instruct his family. Sometimes, by the time his father finished one of the lengthy prayers, Matt was no longer in the room, having crawled off on his knees.

Matt's parents struggled most of their lives to support their children. When the children were old enough to go on missions, however, the money was saved and sacrificed to send them—including Matt. Saying farewell at the train station, Matt's father gave him this last advice, "My boy, you will go out on that mission; you will study;

you will try to prepare your sermons, and sometimes when you are called upon you will think you are wonderfully prepared, but when you stand up, your mind will go completely blank." Matt asked what he should do. Matt's father replied, "You stand up there and with all the fervor of your soul, you bear witness that Joseph Smith was a Prophet of the living God, and thoughts will flood into your mind." Matt later claimed that, his mind being mostly blank during his mission, it gave him the opportunity to often bear testimony from his heart.

On his mission, Matt learned an extra appreciation for those family prayers. He was homesick, thousands of miles from his family. He suffered with boils, tapeworm, skin infections and sunstroke. He would wake up in the morning and find strength knowing that far away his father, mother, sisters and brothers were on their knees praying for him.

After his mission, Matt worked his way through college. Then he made the decision to go to graduate school in Washington, D.C. He found employment to work his way through. By then he was in love with a young woman named Elva. They could not bear to be apart. With limited funds they made plans for Elva to join him. They would be married and live in Washington, D.C. Announcements were printed when Matt's father learned of it. To Matt's father there was only one way for his son to be married, and that was in the temple. There was not a temple in Washington, D.C. at the time, so he must come home to Salt Lake City.

Matt's father had never been good in business and had little to give, yet temple marriage was of such importance to him that he put his faith in God and managed to come up with the money to bring Matt home to be married in the Salt Lake Temple. On July 13, 1922, Matt came home. With Elva they went to the temple to be married for time and all eternity. Accompanied by family members, they entered the East gate of the temple. They all entered, except for Matt's father. The man who had led his son to do what is right, the man whose faith and devotion made the temple marriage possible, did not go in to witness it. He could not go in. He had no recommend, he held no priesthood.

In his adult life, Matt would reminisce, "The greatest sermons of my life were the prayers I heard while a boy in the home of my parents." He would also say, "I was frequently told . . . by our father, that if there ever came a time or an occasion to choose between loyalty to him and loyalty to the priesthood of God, always to choose loyalty to the priesthood of God."

This was especially of significance to Matt's family, for his father, Matthias F. Cowley, had once been a member of the Council of the Twelve, an apostle of the Church. Because of circumstances and divisions, Matthias Cowley resigned the apostleship in 1905, when Matt was a child. But he never ceased to raise his children in the way they should go.

In 1936, President Heber J. Grant, seventh president of The Church of Jesus Christ of Latter-day Saints, welcomed Matthias Cowley back into full fellowship with the Church. Matthias spent his last days doing missionary work in Europe.

And as for his son—Matt, the runaway kid—he translated the *Doctrine and Covenants* and the *Pearl of Great Price* into the Maori language. He revised and reedited the previous translation of the *Book of Mormon*. He courageously served as mission president of the New Zealand Mission during the years of World War II when he had no missionaries but local members and off-duty service men. During this time the mission prospered as never before.

In 1945, Matthew Cowley was called to the Council of the Twelve, standing in the place where his father had served so many years before. He served faithfully in that role till his death in 1953, one of the most loved leaders of his time, a legacy to a faithful father.

Evicted From Their Town

In 1868 southeastern Idaho became an official territory of the U.S. Government. Fifteen years later, in 1883, several Mormon pioneer families banded together and created a town on a tract of forlorn, sage brush-covered land in the new territory. The brush was thick with wood ticks, deer flies, hornets and other pests. Settlers joked that the mosquitoes were large enough to carry away livestock. Indians roamed the land hunting rabbits and deer and befriended the pioneers. They traded and swapped game for supplies.

The desolate land was cleared of brush. Canals were built to irrigate the land. Crude homes were constructed. Wells were dug. Water was transported from the river for culinary use.

The new town was named Rigby. In 1886, an official town site was chosen, a town square was designated, and $20 was paid to the original settler for it. A probate judge was to file on the land in behalf of the settlers. The first school was opened in the one-room community hall. Primitive seats and desks were made. Books were whatever the settlers had. Logs were hewn and hauled. A church was built.

The pioneers were hard-working, dedicated, resourceful and honest. But, unfortunately, they were not lawyers.

One Sunday morning in 1886, the good people of Rigby gathered at the church, only to find that they'd been evicted. All the furnishings had been thrown from the building and a stranger calling himself Jack Robinson stood with a gun in the doorway threatening to kill anyone who tried to enter the church.

It seems that the man was looking for just such an advantageous situation—a town that had been founded on land for which the proper paper work had not been filed. He, in essence, "jumped the claim" and filed declarations of ownership of the town.

Hurried consultations were held. Finally, the pioneers put their scarce cash together and raised $250 to pay off the man. After that they made certain that all the proper legal work for their town was done.

Today Rigby, Idaho has a population of about three thousand 'legal' residents.

The Gospel According to Gibson

T his story has entered the realms of Mormon folklore and been attributed to many sources. One of the earliest sources, and possible originator, is Elder William Gibson, a Scot missionary for The Church of Jesus Christ of Latter-day Saints, who served in Great Britain during the years of 1841-51.

In the early days of the Church, especially in Great Britain, missionaries were expected at public debates. The debates were well attended by people waiting for the opposing sides to point out the errors in each other's doctrine.

At one time a scholarly preacher by the name of the Reverend Mr. Kennedy came to the city of Kilmarnock in central Scotland to debate Elder Gibson. Elder Gibson was well versed in the scriptures and had a gift of speech that enabled him to hold his own against more educated preachers. Mr. Kennedy was a teacher of Latin, Hebrew and Greek and therefore acquainted with the Biblical scriptures in their earlier forms. Elder Gibson had no such education, but he did have a gift of common sense. Mr. Kennedy had a theatrical flair. In an early debate with a Mormon missionary, he had angrily thrown the Book of Mormon on the floor of the platform and demonstratively stamped on it. When he proposed to challenge Elder Gibson, a crowd of people came to attend what promised to be a colorful debate. So many people attended that the debate had to be held in the largest hall in the city.

Mr. Kennedy arrived at the debate armed with religious tomes, Bible dictionaries and scriptures in the ancient languages. All Elder Gibson had was his little pocket-sized King James Bible, and the faith that the Lord would make the gospel plain to the honest in heart.

The topic for that evening's debate was the "Correct Mode of Baptism." Mr. Kennedy began the debate. He started by insulting the mental capabilities of Mormons and giving proof that, if it were not so, Elder Gibson would not attempt to debate so illustrious and learned an expert as himself. He said that it was because of the ignorance of Mormons that they did not know how to interpret the teachings of the Bible and that he, Mr. Kennedy, would take the same passages Mormon preachers used to prove that "immersion" was the proper form of baptism and prove that those passages didn't mean what the Mormons said at all.

"I will begin," said Mr. Kennedy, "with Matthew 3:16: 'And Jesus, when he was baptized, went straightway out of the water.' Now, my opponent, being an ignoramus, will likely argue this way: 'He could not have come out of the water unless he had first gone down into it, and if pouring or sprinkling is the right mode of baptism, there would have been no occasion for him to have done so. This passage, then, shows that he must have been immersed. Very fine logic, but entirely wrong. It is well known that the New Testament was translated from the Greek. Now, the words OUT OF in the Greek have not the same meaning that we in our language apply to them. They merely mean FROM a place, never supposing that the person was IN but only AT the place. To prove this I will quote another passage found in Acts 12:10. It is the account of the deliverance of Peter from prison by an angel. In the tenth verse it says the angel departed FROM Peter. Now, if any gentleman will come upon the platform, it does not matter whether he understands Greek or not, I will show him that the Greek characters here translated FROM are the very same which in Matthew are translated OUT OF, and as we cannot suppose the angel to be IN Peter, but only AT or BESIDE him, then Jesus was not IN the water, but only AT or BESIDE it."

Mr. Kennedy was applauded for his reasoning. He continued. "I will now turn to what is thought the strongest language in the New Testament in favor of immersion. It is the account of the baptism of the eunuch by Philip, found in Acts 8:38,39. Here we find the words INTO the water and OUT OF the water, but unfortunately for my opponent and others like him, the word INTO used here is liable to the same objection as the word OUT OF in the original Greek. It only means to come TO a place. The real translation of this passage is, 'They came TO the water and he baptized him; then they went FROM the water.'"

Mr. Kennedy was again applauded for his scholarship. He went on to say that he could prove that sprinkling was the correct mode of cleansing by quoting from Numbers 19. He read verses 18, 20 and half of 19, as if the other half of the verse did not exist. He again derided Elder Gibson for not knowing his scriptures.

Then it was Elder Gibson's turn. He replied as follows: "I have, my friends, been called an ignoramus, and if ignorance of Greek and Hebrew makes a man an ignoramus, then I am one, for I do not know anything about them. But God has been kind to me in giving me a little of that which is generally called common sense. I cannot test Mr. Kennedy's assertions by Greek or Hebrew, so I shall have to bring them to the simpler test of that sense of which I have spoken.

"But first, I wish to give my friend a bit of advice. For years he has been telling his congregation in Paisley and other places that the Scriptures of the Old and New Testament are the words of God, and those who will not believe them as such will go to hell. Now, I advise him to tell his congregation that he has found out that the Scriptures are not translated correctly and cannot be understood without a knowledge of Greek and Hebrew; therefore, as his congregations are, even as I, a set of ignoramuses, they need not believe the Scriptures as written. Though the Bible says that the commandments of God are so plain that he who runs may read, and so simple that any man, though a fool, cannot err therein, yet without a knowledge of the dead languages people cannot understand even how to get baptized.

"Let us see now how your Greek logic will agree with common sense. We will take Matthew 3:16 first, where it is said that Jesus, when he was baptized, came up out of the water. Mr. Kennedy says that in the Greek, this does not mean OUT OF, but merely FROM, and FROM does not presuppose that he was IN but only AT the water. To prove this, Acts 12:10 is quoted where it says the angel departed FROM Peter; and then it is declared that the character which is translated FROM in Acts is the very same that is rendered OUT OF in Matthew. We are told that we cannot believe that the angel was INSIDE Peter, but only AT or BESIDE him.

"What a pity to spoil such fine logic. It is almost as good as proving that a horse chestnut is a chestnut horse. Why not, when the same character is in both terms? Let us apply Mr. Kennedy's rule of interpretation to Acts 12:17: 'But he beckoning unto them with the hand to hold their peace, declared unto them how the Lord had brought them OUT of prison.' Now, if Peter had had Mr. Kennedy with him, Mr. Kennedy could have proved to Peter from the Greek that OUT OF does not mean OUT OF, but only FROM; and FROM never supposed he was IN the prison, but only AT or BESIDE it, perhaps just looking in at the gateway, when the angel came and led him away.

"Now, let us consider his assertion about the word INTO. He declared that this word in the New Testament does not mean INTO but only TO a place, or BESIDE it. How will this apply to Matthew 25:41: 'Then shall he say also unto them on the left hand, Depart from me, ye cursed, INTO everlasting fire, prepared for the devil and his angels.' Mr. Kennedy's Greek logic comes in very handy here. By it he has proved that immersion is not the proper mode of baptism, but that it is by sprinkling, and, therefore, by the same reasoning, this passage of Scripture means that the wicked are not to go INTO the fire, but only TO it, and be sprinkled with the brimstone.

"Let us consider Mr. Kennedy's assertion that there is no such thing as immersion in all the law of Moses, but that all cleansing was done by sprinkling. To prove this, Numbers 19 was quoted, and verses 18 and 20 were read. The latter part of the nineteenth was missed. Now, Mr. Kennedy, why did you omit that? Was it because you wished to deceive this audience? The part you omitted to read in this quotation reads, 'And on the seventh day he shall purify himself, and wash his clothes, and bathe himself IN water, and he shall be clean at even."

At this point, Mr. Kennedy arose and stated that he refused to discuss the subject with Elder Gibson any longer. The entertained crowd soon broke up, and there was no question concerning who was the victor in that debate.

Parley and the Bull Dog

Parley P. Pratt was one of the first missionaries for the restored church. In the 1830's he traveled on foot preaching to both the Indians and the white settlers on the frontiers of what was the new America.

While on a mission in Ohio, Parley met with persecution against what was perceived as a radical new church. One night he stopped at the home of Simeon Carter, about fifty miles west of Kirtland. While in the house, an officer named Peabody entered and arrested him. Parley was taken in the dark over muddy roads about two miles to a place of trial. As the proceedings appeared farcical to Parley, he made no answer to their ridiculous charges.

In his autobiography Parley recounted, "I was soon ordered to prison or to pay a sum of money which I had not in the world. It was now a late hour and I was still retained in court, tantalized, abused and urged to settle the matter, to all of which I made no reply. This greatly exhausted their patience. It was near midnight. I now called on Brother Peterson to sing a hymn in the court. We sang 'O, how happy are they.' This exasperated them still more, and they pressed us greatly to settle the business by paying the money.

"I then observed as follows: 'May it please the court, I have one proposal to make for a final settlement of the things that seem to trouble you. It is this: If the witnesses who have given testimony in the case will repent of their false swearing, and the magistrate of his unjust and wicked judgment, and of his persecution, blackguardism, and abuse, and all kneel down together, we will pray for you, that God might forgive you in these matters.'"

The so-called "court" did not react favorably to Parley's suggestions. Parley was sentenced to a local prison to serve time until he came up with the money. The meeting was broken up.

The prison was a few miles away and, as it was late at night, Parley was taken to a nearby public house and locked in till morning when he would be escorted by Officer Peabody to the prison.

In the morning Officer Peabody took Parley to breakfast, then they sat waiting till the transportation and arrangements were ready. Wrote Parley, "After sitting awhile by the fire, in charge of the officer, I requested to step out. I walked out into the public square, accompanied by him. Said I, 'Mr. Peabody, are you good at a race?' 'No,' said he, 'but my big bull dog is, and he has been trained to assist me in my office these several years; he will take any man down at my bidding.'

"Well, Mr. Peabody," said Parley, "you compelled me to go a mile, I have gone with you two miles. You have given me an opportunity to preach, sing, and have entertained me with lodging and breakfast. I must now go on my journey; if you are good at a race, you can accompany me. I thank you for all your kindness—good day, sir."

"I then started on my journey, while he stood amazed, and not able to step one foot before the other. Seeing this, I halted, turned to him and again invited him to a race. He still stood amazed. I then renewed my exertions and soon increased my speed to something like that of a deer. He did not awaken from his astonishment sufficiently to engage in pursuit till I had gained, perhaps, two hundred yards. I had already leaped a fence, and was making my way through a field to a forest on the right of the road. He now came hallowing after me, and shouting to his dog to seize me. The dog, being one of the largest I ever saw, came close on my footsteps with all his fury; the officer behind, still in pursuit, clapping his hands and hallowing 'Stu-boy, stu-boy—take him, Watch—lay hold of him. I say, down with him,' and pointing his finger in the direction I was running.

"The dog was fast overtaking me, and in the act of leaping upon me, when, quick as lightning, the thought struck me, to assist the officer in sending the dog with all fury to the forest a little distance before me. I pointed my finger in that direction, clapped my hands, and shouted in imitation of the officer.

Upon hearing Parley give the same command, the dog redoubled his speed and hastened past Parley and into the forest, leaving the officer far behind. Parley then directed his path to meet with his companions.

Parley P. Pratt added a note to this story. Simeon Carter, disturbed by the incident, sought to find evidence against Parley. When Parley had been arrested, he had dropped his Book of Mormon and Carter still had possession of it. Simeon Carter read the book with attention. It was not what he had supposed it to be and the words wrought deeply upon his mind. After reading the book, Carter traveled fifty miles to Kirtland where he was baptized and ordained an Elder.

Rebel with a Cause

Many are the heroes, artists and writers despised in their own time, only to be revered later. It seems that every age is shocked by new music. While most new songs are lost in time, some live on to become classics. When Johann Strauss, Sr. popularized the waltz in dance and music, he was condemned and disparaged from pulpits and podiums for the scandalous, radical fad. Years later he was honored as father of a classical dance and music style. When Elvis Presley introduced his brand of rock-and-roll, he was decried from pulpits throughout his country. Yet today his style is considered conservative.

This is the story of another rebel. His name was James Montgomery. He lived in the times of Joseph Smith, but he lived in another country. He wrote songs and poetry that were considered seditious. His sentiments disturbed the status quo. He was criticized by both the government and the churches.

At sixteen he was apprenticed to a grocer but ran away. He began writing poetry and songs at age nineteen but could find no one to publish them. So strongly did he feel about his songs, however, that he entered the publishing profession in hopes of someday seeing his works in print. He finally found work with a revolutionary newspaper, the *Sheffield Register*, which shared his views on social reform. The owner had to flee to America to avoid imprisonment, which enabled James to take over the paper himself. He renamed it the *Sheffield Iris*. He published the paper for three decades, till 1825. During that time, however, he met with much antagonism from the government and churches. He was imprisoned. He was fined. He was convicted of sedition. Still, he kept it up.

It was not until James was an old man that his writings, songs and poems on social and religious reform were finally accepted.

He retired an influential and popular man. The government that had prosecuted him supported him in his old age with a pension in gratitude for his works. But earlier in his life it was not so. He was persecuted as a radical. He wrote four hundred hymns and poems, most of which have faded from popularity and memory.

One song, a hit of its time, might have been forgotten today if it had not been for an incident in LDS Church history. The song might have been interpreted by some as a condemnation of those who did not empathize with and aid the poor, the sick, the prisoner. Some Mormons, however, found the song a comfort.

On June 27, 1844, four men sat in a jail in Carthage, Illinois. Joseph was low in spirits. To cheer him, John Taylor sang to him one of the prophet's favorite songs, a modern song by James Montgomery. When the song was over, Taylor was asked to sing it again. Taylor sang again of the poor wayfaring man of grief, the want, the thirst, the injustice done to him. He sang, "In pris'n I saw him next, condemned to meet a traitor's doom at morn. The tide of lying tongues I stemmed, and honored him 'mid shame and scorn. My friendship's utmost zeal to try, he asked if I for him would die. The flesh was weak; my blood ran chill, but my free spirit cried, 'I will!'"

While Taylor sang the song, a mob was gathering. Two hours later Joseph and his brother Hyrum were murdered for their beliefs.

James Montgomery wrote, "He spake, and my poor name he named, 'Of me thou hast not been ashamed. These deeds shall thy memorial be; Fear not, thou didst them unto me.'"

The incident in 1844 sealed the song forever in the hearts of Latter-day Saints.

Another of James's songs, a poem set to varying music and finally set to music by George Careless for the LDS hymnal, was James's answer to many religious officials of his time. Educated clerics argued that only a well-educated man who understood the ways of deity and the order of heaven could know how to pray in a precise and formal manner. Prayer was an art and a science and must be learned by studying carefully all the laws of prayer. James answered these church officials with a song containing his own radical ideas about what prayer was:

Prayer is the soul's sincere desire, uttered or unexpressed, The motion of a hidden fire that trembles in the breast. Prayer is the burden of a sigh, the falling of a tear, The upward glancing of an eye when none but God is near. Prayer is the simplest form of speech that infant lips can try; prayer, the sublimest strains that reach the Majesty on high. Prayer is the Christian's vital breath, the Christian's native air, His watchword at the gates of death; he enters heav'n with prayer.

Though time has dimmed the memory of most of James Montgomery's works, Latter-day Saints still honor the rebel with a cause.

The Promised Babe

When Margaret McMurrin put her hand to a handcart, she did not loosen her grip till she'd pulled a thousand miles. A thousand miles . . . and more. In the new Zion, young Margaret married Samuel. The two moved on to settle desert country. They lived in homes of scarce wood, clay, and dirt floors. In this wilderness Margaret cried in pain of birth, then wept in grief of death as her still-born babe was taken from her. There were no hospitals, no sterile rooms, no pain-relieving drugs, only the comforts of sisters who understood her pain. Again Margaret risked her life in the wilderness to bring forth birth. That child too was born in death.

Years passed, bringing more innocent spirits, each to receive a body only soon to pass back through the veil. Ten times frail Margaret laid herself in the valley of the shadow of death. Ten times the babes were stillborn or lived only minutes after birth. Her heart cried out for the blessings of a living child. Burdened with unimaginable grief, Margaret would not give up her faith.

Samuel and Margaret made the long, difficult trek from the Panaca, Nevada settlement to Salt Lake City where Patriarch Abel Lamb gave Margaret a blessing. The blessing said, ". . . you shall have a son and he shall be a mighty man in Israel and his name shall be the name of his father's; therefore trust in the Lord and have faith in His promises and it shall be fulfilled every whit and the blessing of Sarah of old shall be conferred upon thee . . . ." Sarah of old was the wife of Abraham. She was barren and past childbearing when God granted her one son. That one son became the father of the Israelite nation. Such a thing did not seem possible to Margaret, just as it had not seemed possible to faithful Sarah.

Samuel and Margaret returned to the desert settlement. For the eleventh time Margaret laid down her life on the birthing bed. Again a babe was stillborn. Again Margaret cried out to God and comforted herself that this was the trial of her faith.

In 1875, Margaret risked her life for the twelfth and last time. It was the final sacrifice. Prematurely born and not expected to live, the babe of promise laid by his mother as her life slipped away, as if in exchange. One life for another. The twelfth child, a son, was the only one to live.

The babe, Samuel, was named for his father. He weighed only three-and-a-half pounds and was so tiny a large finger ring could be slipped over his arm. Born into a world hostile to premature births, Samuel nevertheless survived.

Samuel grew to manhood, married, and had a son. That son's name was Harold Bingham Lee, who also grew to manhood and became eleventh President of The Church of Jesus Christ of Latter-day Saints.

Frontier M.D.

D r. Ellis Shipp was about the best bone-setter in the pioneering West.

As a youngster, Ellis would accompany Grandpa William Hawley in his buggy while on his rounds to set broken limbs. Little Ellis was fascinated by Grandpa Hawley's heavy black medical bag and the work he did with it. In later years Ellis would say, "I learned more from Grandfather about setting bones than I did in medical college."

Life on the frontier was difficult: the goal of higher education was a dream subjected to the struggles for survival. It was not till Ellis was twenty-eight that, with the support and encouragement of family and of President Brigham Young, the first step was taken toward a medical degree. Ellis traveled to Philadelphia and, as some other Utahns had done, enrolled in the medical school there. Funds from home soon dwindled. To stay in school Ellis had to take part-time jobs, summer jobs, even a job at the college as night guard for the hall of cadavers. Finally Ellis earned the degree of Doctor of Medicine and graduated with high honors. Returning to Utah, a medical practice was set up specializing in minor surgery, obstetrics and diseases.

In 1879, Dr. Shipp, determined to improve adequate medical help throughout the West, founded a school to teach medical and health-care techniques. Through the years some five hundred students, from all over the West, were trained at the school. Graduates took the regular territorial examinations for health-care licenses. Dr. Shipp's influence on improving medicine in the pioneering territory was unparalleled.

Dr. Shipp continued to practice and teach till almost ninety years of age. Throughout an amazing career, Dr. Shipp continued to study and keep abreast of medical developments, even returning East for additional training—at colleges that would allow the good doctor to attend. Though Ellis was one of the best-educated physicians in Utah, many Eastern medical colleges would not accept Ellis—because Ellis was a woman. Yet, because of her talent and intelligence, her advice was often sought by male colleagues—even though the doors of many eastern hospitals were closed to her.

Of Dr. Shipp's five hundred students, all were women, training for licenses in midwifery and nursing, and returning to their own communities with these skills. In addition, Dr. Shipp traveled to remote settlements in Canada, Mexico, Arizona, Idaho, and points all over the West to offer workshops in basic medical care. Dr. Shipp, along with her Mormon sister doctors such as Dr. Romania Pratt Penrose, Dr. Martha Hughes Cannon, Dr. Ellen Brooke Ferguson, Dr. Margaret Curtis Shipp, Dr. Jennie Scholfield, Dr. Margaret C. Roberts, Dr. Elvira S. Barney, Dr. Emma Atkin, Dr. Jane Ivins McDonald, Dr. Mary Green Van Schoonhooven, Dr. Elsie Ada Faust, Dr. Belle Anderson Gemmel and others, were not only pioneers bringing health care to the West, they were pioneering women in their field. In their time the Utah Territory had the nation's largest per capita concentration of women doctors. Their work left a tremendous legacy that has remained to this day.

Speaking of the difficulties of frontier medicine, Dr. Ralph T. Richards stated in his book, *Of Medicine, Hospitals, and Doctors*, "Mention has already been made of the urgent need . . . for trained nurses and midwives. No one did more toward solving this problem than Dr. Ellis R. Shipp . . . unquestionably the outstanding woman of her time. . . . The West owes her a debt of gratitude."

Emergency at the Virgin Ditch

Alegend from Holland tells of the courageous little Dutch boy who saved the dike by sticking his finger into the leak. Early Mormon pioneers can boast of a similar story.

When Mormon pioneers settled the southern Utah area known as Dixie, they built irrigation ditches to bring water to the desert soil. Without irrigation, no crops could be raised on the arid land. The ditches were imperative to survival in that hostile wilderness. One of the main sources of water was the Virgin River.

A long, deep ditch was dug to divert water from the river to the settlements. It was called the Virgin Ditch. Because of the elements, gophers, and occasional floods, the earthen walls of the Virgin Ditch were continually patrolled. One break in the earthen walls could wash away an entire section of the vital ditch.

In 1864, Brigham Jarvis was patrolling the Virgin Ditch, taking his assigned turn. Jarvis had been patrolling for two days and nights, mending breaks and cracks, only stopping for one meal. His father, George Jarvis, had joined him when they came upon a breach in the ditch wall. Water had begun to pour through, melting the wall around it. With shovel and spade the men furiously flung gravel and earth against the breach. They made no progress. As fast as earth was thrown, the escaping water washed it away.

The break was close to the home of a local Indian named Buck Hairlip. He saw what was happening and came to help the Jarvises. But even the three men could not stop the break. The earthen wall had lost five feet of bank and the vital ditch was in danger of going all together. Then Buck Hairlip called to his wife, Sally.

Sally emerged from the Indian home. Sally was built on a generous scale. She was wide around the veranda. Nature had not been the least bit stingy with her form.

As the Jarvises watched this formidably large woman walking toward them, they heard her talking in her native tongue in what they took to be angry tones, and feared her. But it was not as they had supposed. When Sally reached the ditch, she lowered herself into the breach and plugged up the hole. She stayed there for some time while the men shoveled dirt against her ample back side and rebuilt the wall. The ditch and the pioneer crops were saved.

Now, the Dutch can brag about the dike being saved by a little boy's finger, but the Mormons can brag about the ditch being saved by the back side of a good woman.

The Big Mine

Erastus and his wife joined The Church of Jesus Christ of Latter-day Saints in 1833. First living in Vermont, Erastus and his family moved with the Saints to Kirtland, then to Missouri, then to Illinois. Erastus came west to Utah in 1847 with the wagon trains.

In 1850 Brigham Young located the city of Ogden in an old mountain-men gathering area. Here Erastus chose the site for his farm. In 1851, Erastus was ordained a bishop to preside over the Saints on the north side of the Ogden River. He also served in the Territorial Legislature. He was an influential and well-loved man.

This story involves what happened to Erastus and his family from the time he arrived in the Salt Lake Valley in 1847 till the time he moved to Ogden.

One son, Erastus, Jr., was in the Mormon Battalion (part of the U.S. Army) that went to California. He returned to Utah. Then news came from other Battalion members of the gold discoveries in California. Erastus, Jr. itched to go to the gold fields. Brigham Young advised that it was all right if the gold was used to build up the Kingdom of God. Erastus, Jr. traveled to California but, alas, was unsuccessful and returned home to Utah.

Two other sons, Sanford and Thomas, also had an itch for mining, but they stayed in Utah. When Erastus was granted grazing rights in a Utah canyon, Sanford, Thomas, and Sanford's wife, Martha Ann, herded cattle there. As Sanford, Martha Ann and Thomas herded, they threw stones at straying cattle. Some of the rocks they threw were heavier than others. They brought the rocks in and had the ore tested. The ore tested for gold, silver and copper. Lots of copper. It was promising ore. Right there in Utah. But in those early years the Saints were struggling to survive and had few resources. Brigham Young advised them not to pursue mining, but to pursue greater things.

The family dedicated themselves to building up the Kingdom instead of building up a mining empire. That is when they went on to help found the city of Ogden, Utah.

The canyon where ore was found was not forgotten. It was named Bingham Canyon in honor of Erastus Bingham and his family. Soon others came and mined the ore the Bingham family had discovered and left behind. The largest open pit mine in the world today, Bingham Copper Mine, is up Bingham Canyon.

In 1949, a century after the discovery of the ore, a monument was erected in Bingham Canyon to the memory of the Bingham family, the family that had more important things to do than mine.

The Non-Mormon
Who Saved Nauvoo

M ajor Lewis C. Bidamon, a Virginian, moved to Nauvoo in April, 1846. Though he was not a Mormon, he was immediately caught up in sympathy because of the persecutions they were undergoing. His sense of justice was outraged at the murders, pillagings and mobbings.

At one time a mobocrat army was forming around Nauvoo, poised to take the city in a massacre. Bidamon tried talking with the mob leaders to dissuade them of their purposes. One of the mob leaders, Thomas C. Sharp, told Bidamon that because he was sympathetic to the Mormons, he was considered a "Jack Mormon," and that if he did not pull back, he would share the same fate as the Mormons. When Bidamon described the sufferings of the women and children of Nauvoo, Sharp said, "Drive the women into the river and throw their damned young ones in after them."

Feeling an attack on the city was imminent, non-Mormon citizens in Nauvoo gathered and appointed Major Bidamon to negotiate with the mobbers for peace. They also urged him to make his way to Governor Ford to plead for help.

Bidamon left Nauvoo for Springfield, but just outside of Nauvoo came under attack by the piratical mobbers. He was lucky to escape with his life. Leading citizens of neighboring towns and law officers attempted to get through but also were attacked and shot at by the lawless mob.

Bidamon fought his way out, made his way to the relative safety of Quincy, and was on the last leg of his trip to Springfield when he stopped in Mount Sterling a few hours for rest. He was surrounded by citizens in Mount Sterling who were curious to know about the situation in Nauvoo. Bidamon told about the impending violence there. A hard-looking, unkempt man came up to Bidamon saying that he was a captain in a militia, and he was going to Nauvoo the next day. In spite of the man's words, his piratical manners told Bidamon what the man really was and what kind of militia he belonged to. It suddenly occurred to Bidamon that he could use this man. He asked the man if he would carry a letter for him to his brother in Nauvoo. The man said he would on condition that he knew the contents of the letter. Bidamon agreed. He wrote a few lines, advising the citizens of Nauvoo to refrain from shedding blood . . . if possible. He continued to write, "for it would be an easy matter for you with your hell acres and hell half acres to destroy the whole mob force at once."

"What do you mean by hell acres and hell half acres?" demanded the scruffy man.

"Oh, I don't like to tell you that," said Bidamon.

The man swore and ejaculated, "I will not carry your letter."

"Very well," said Bidamon. "Provided you can keep a secret, I will explain to you."

The man said he could keep a secret, so Bidamon proceeded to tell him that every approach to Nauvoo was undermined with large quantities of explosive powder deposited in such a manner that by the pulling of certain wires, mechanically arranged, it could be exploded at will.

None of what Bidamon said was true about the "hell acres," but it bought precious time that saved many lives. He learned later that indeed his letter had been taken to the mob camp and read. The mob, although strong enough to have taken Nauvoo at that time, concluded to wait for more marauding reinforcements, giving both the Mormon and non-Mormon citizens of Nauvoo time for negotiations, legal reinforcements and necessary supplies for the Mormons to leave Nauvoo. Nauvoo was saved—for a while.

Sympathetic non-Mormon citizens contributed supplies to ease the sufferings of the Mormons and help them escape Nauvoo with a minimal loss of lives. But even with the Mormons gone, the city was pillaged and homes ransacked and torched, including homes of the non-Mormons who lived there.

Bidamon escaped several murder attempts and lived to testify against Governor Ford for not sending legal help to stop the rioting horde of plunderers.

Bidamon returned to Nauvoo, where his own home had been pillaged. He, along with the other remaining citizens of Nauvoo, began to rebuild.

In 1847, Major Bidamon married Emma Hale Smith, widow of the Prophet Joseph Smith. In his later years he welcomed to his home traveling Mormons visiting the site of so much of their history. Bidamon never joined the LDS Church, but at least two of his grandchildren did.

The Unloved Woman

B orn in 1828, Emmeline was a precocious child. She went to school and earned her teaching certificate by the age of fourteen. At fourteen she also discovered a wonderful thing—the gospel of Jesus Christ. She was baptized that year into The Church of Jesus Christ of Latter-day Saints in the icy waters of a Massachusetts stream. At her baptism, schoolmates, ministers and curiosity seekers came to jeer at her for her choice. Her friends turned against her. The only love and support she felt were from her mother and her God.

At age fifteen, Emmeline fell in love with James Harris, a fifteen-year-old Mormon boy. It was, she wrote in later life, the only true "love match" she would know. They shared ideals, faith and tender passions.

The two idealistic youngsters traveled to Nauvoo by steamship where Emmeline met the prophet Joseph Smith and secured a testimony of his divine calling, a testimony that she could never deny. A few months after her coming to Nauvoo, Joseph Smith and his brother Hyrum were murdered in Carthage, Illinois. The fledgling church suffered confusion and increasingly serious persecution from outsiders.

Emmeline bore James a son. But unable to endure the persecution, James left Emmeline, saying he would come back for her. James's mother went to Nauvoo and tried to steal Emmeline's baby. The baby died, and James's mother intended that Emmeline would never see James again. Yet Emmeline did not give up hope in James's promises. She waited and watched as boat after boat docked at Nauvoo. She wrote in her diary, "Last night there came a steamboat up the river. Oh, how my youthful heart fluttered with hope, with anxiety. My limbs were affected to that degree. I was obliged to lay aside my work. I rely upon the promises he has made me and not all that has been said can shake my confidence in the only man I ever loved . . . I watched the boat . . . I saw a person approaching. My heart beat with fond anticipation. It walked like James. He came nearer and just as I was about to speak his name he spoke and I found I was deceived by the darkness. . . . I am alone." She had been married little more than a year when she was abandoned.

Emmeline was young, physically tiny even for her age, destitute, inexperienced, and grieving for a lost child. She was alone in a world where women were primarily dependent on the protections and support of men, deserted by the one she trusted and loved. She was plunged into the depths of sorrow and illness. On her sickbed she was given a blessing. It was a blessing amazing for one so young. In the blessing was said, "You will live to do a work that has never been done by any woman, since the creation."

Emmeline recovered. She was taken into the home of Elizabeth Ann and Newel K. Whitney, an older couple influential in the Church. They treated her with much love and consideration. The principle of plural marriage had been introduced in the Church. Elizabeth talked with Emmeline about it, about the security to be found in this time of change when the only defense a woman had against society was her family. Emmeline married Newel K. Whitney in 1845. He was thirty-three years her senior. In later years, Emmeline would write that Newel K. Whitney was "as good a man as ever lived, a father to all within his reach and more than father to me.

The Whitney family traveled west to Utah. Emmeline bore two daughters. After five years, Newel K. Whitney died and the family was again thrown into disarray and without a protector. Still young, and with two babies, Emmeline searched desperately for a stable environment. She was attracted to Daniel H. Wells, a counselor to Brigham Young and mayor of Salt Lake City. He already had five wives and their children to support. Still, she saw in him a secure

situation. Emmeline did what was certainly rare in those times —
she proposed to him. In a letter, she laid her feelings bare and told
how much she esteemed him. She impressed upon him his duty to
care for women, especially herself, since he had been Newel K.
Whitney's friend.

There is no record that Daniel ever promised Emmeline more
than a practical union. He was not in love with her. Out of a sense
of spiritual and social obligation, he offered only his support and
protection as part of his family. Emmeline desired it. At the age of
twenty-four she became the sixth wife of Daniel H. Wells. He was
thirty-eight.

Daniel Wells owned a mansion in Salt Lake City to house his
large family, but there was no room for Emmeline and her daughters,
so he procured a small house for her nearby.

Emmeline finally enjoyed some financial security. But it was not
enough for her romantic nature. She craved for more. She wanted her
husband to love her. Daniel did his duty by her, but it was not enough
for her. In her diary she wrote, "My husband came, my heart gave
one great bound towards him; O how enthusiastically I love him;
truly and devotedly if he could only feel towards me in any degree
as I do towards him how happy it would make me." Daniel did his
duty by her and she bore three daughters to him, two of whom died
as young women.

Emmeline tried to become closer to the entire Wells family. She
wanted a mutually satisfying relationship with Daniel's other wives.
She wrote letters pleading for their love and companionship. Her letters were mostly ignored.

Others of the wives were gifted in the skills of high society.
Emmeline was not. Others of the wives were gifted in the skills of
homemaking. Emmeline was not. She preferred late nights of stimu-
lating conversation to mastering the womanly skills of home management. Emmeline did not fit with the other wives. Other wives
wore current fashions. Emmeline, only five feet tall and weighing

barely a hundred pounds wore dresses in romantic pastels, even in winter, instead of dignified darker colors. She wore scarves and earrings and rings on her fingers. Her "quaint" dress was a source of merriment to some.

When parties were held at the Wells mansion, Emmeline was not included. When Daniel hosted dignitaries, another wife, not Emmeline, was always chosen as hostess. At social events, another wife was always chosen as Daniel's escort, not Emmeline. Once Emmeline recalled visiting the theater only to see Daniel there. They passed each other politely, showing not a sign of recognition and her heart wept and hoped that someday she too would be an acknowledged love. She wrote in her diary, "O if only my husband could only love me even a little and not seem to be perfectly indifferent to any sensation of that kind, he cannot know the craving of my nature, he is surrounded with love on every side, and I am cast out . . . . "

Emmeline wrote love poems to Daniel, but two of the wives got hold of them and ridiculed and teased her. From Daniel and others of the wives she received only a distant respect and friendship.

Years passed. Beloved daughters died. Off and on Emmeline suffered tremendous bouts of depression that kept her bedridden. She suffered fits of uncontrolled sobbing. She suffered feelings of loneliness cured only by loved company and long, enlivening conversation. Still her passionate nature cried for more. Still her diary was filled with notes of sorrow and of unrequited love. "This evening I fully expected my husband here but was again disappointed . . . He is not in want of me for a companion or in any sense, he does not need me at all . . . I am shut out of his life . . . I am held at such a distance."

This was romantic Emmeline's cross to bear—never to have a great love of her life.

This was Emmeline's life, but not her only life. Emmeline was gifted. Through the years of adversity, she learned to rely on herself and her God. She learned independence. She became outspoken, sometimes to the point of brusqueness. She gave her daughters superior educations and taught them skills they needed to survive in a world that was not always protecting and loving. She was a contributing writer to the *Woman's Exponent*, the first major publication for women west of the Mississippi, a publication begun by Lula Greene Richards and backed by Eliza R. Snow, Brigham Young and other church leaders. In 1871, Emmeline assumed editorship, a position in which she served for forty-three years. She advocated for women's education, health care, self esteem, the right to have an opinion, the right to legal recognition, the right to enter the work place if need be, the right to survive without being dependent on men, the right of women to be acknowledged as a people in their own right. She argued that if the government trusted women with the 'right' and obligation to pay taxes, women had the "right" to vote where those taxes went.

Emmeline influenced thought on women's rights throughout the Utah territory as well as becoming a powerful voice in the East and in Britain. She was befriended by leaders of the U.S. suffrage movement such as Elizabeth Cady Stanton and Susan B. Anthony. Even though many women in the suffrage movement slighted Emmeline for her religion, Stanton and Anthony stood by her as a valuable addition to the cause.

Back in 1842, Emmeline's surrogate mother and sister wife, Elizabeth Ann Whitney, had been a charter member and counselor in the formation of the "Relief Society," an organization begun by Joseph Smith for the development and empowerment of women, one of the first independent women's organizations created. Following in her beloved "Mother Whitney's" footsteps, Emmeline, decades later, was named General Secretary of the Relief Society in which capacity she served for twenty years.

During this time, Brigham Young approached General Secretary Emmeline with a prophetic call, which she took as a solemn entrustment. Brigham told her to save wheat. And save wheat she did.

Sisters of the Relief Society all over the territory saved grain to fill the Relief Society silos and storehouses. Some wheat was used to help the poor. But most of the wheat was saved, saved for an event that none of them could foresee.

In 1879, because of her involvement with the women's suffrage movement, then president of the church, John Taylor, appointed Emmeline a delegate to Washington, D.C. to represent Mormon women. With the support of her Church, of the Relief Society, and of her husband, she fulfilled her calling. She lobbied U.S. presidents on behalf of the rights of Mormon women and of women everywhere. She helped to soften attitudes toward her Church in a time when it was politically unpopular. She participated in and held offices and delegate status in the National Women's Suffrage, American Women's Suffrage and International Women's Suffrage movements.

At Church expense she traveled, even to Britain, giving speeches and writing and contributing her influence to the cause of women's rights. Her own publication was distributed to far corners of the world. She saw women of the Utah territory granted the vote in 1870, only to see it taken away in 1887, not to be reinstated till Utah achieved statehood in 1896.

She became a 'behind the scenes' influence in Utah politics, as well as a forefront debater for women's rights. Many in the LDS Church were divided as to what constituted women's rights. The Church advocated family and child-bearing as women's primary priorities, and it supported education for women. But some felt that women were going too far in their demands. Elder B.H. Roberts opposed women's right to vote and became an adversary of Emmeline in speech and print. It wasn't till years later they resolved their differences and Elder Roberts accorded Emmeline the honors of a great woman.

She had come a long way from being a lonely girl, love-sick and destitute. She had taken the self-pitying feelings of unrequited love, she had taken her passions and griefs, and she had channeled them into causes that made a difference in the world.

Emmeline reached her early sixties as a responsible, independent and influential woman when things began to change in her personal life. Daniel was in his late seventies, nearing the end of a long life spent in service and sacrifice to his Church. He had been apart from Emmeline for a long time, but his attitude now seemed changed toward her. He sought out the company of his quaintly-dressed little wife. In her diary she again poured out her feelings. "O the joy of being once more in his dear presence—his room is so nice and we are so cozy by the large grate and such a comfortable fire in it. We are more like lovers than husband and wife for we are so far removed from each other there is always the embarrassment of lovers and yet we have been married more than 37 years—how odd it seems I do not feel old neither does he—we are young to each other and that is well."

Their late-life romance was short lived. In 1891, Emmeline and other family members were called to the beside of Daniel H. Wells where he passed away.

In the mid-1890's, the practice of plural marriage was phased out of Church practice. Women were now facing a kinder world in which to survive independently should the ideal of perfect marriage fail them in this life.

Over the years, Relief Society General Secretary Emmeline stayed true to Brigham Young's calling to save wheat. The women of the Relief Society continued to save wheat, selling it only to buy new wheat to keep the granaries fresh. Some laughed at the sisters and criticized their holding back perfectly good wheat. Wrote Emmeline, "We have been ridiculed more over this than over any other one thing in the Relief Society."

Some bishops began confiscating the wheat from the Relief Society, selling it for building funds, priesthood projects, or whatever good purposes they had in mind. President John Taylor and his counselors learned of the confiscations. Reinforcing Brigham Young's prophecy that there would come a time for the wheat, the First Presidency issued letters to all bishops that the wheat belonged to those who had collected it, the Relief Society, and only they would know when the time came to release it.

A famine came to China and the Relief Society sent a train car load of grain. The great earthquake hit San Francisco and the Relief Society sent a train car load of wheat. The bulk of the wheat, however, stayed and the Relief Society kept saving.

In October 1910, when Emmeline reached the age of eighty-three, she received yet another calling from her Church. She was asked by the Relief Society presiding committee as well as Mormon Church President Joseph F. Smith, if she would serve as President of the Relief Society. Emmeline had expected someone younger to be called to the fill the position and questioned if at her age she had the strength for it. She was their choice, however, and she accepted.

In 1912, at eighty-four years of age, Emmeline was presented with an honorary doctorate degree from Brigham Young University, a rare honor in a country whose leading institutions still did not consider women worthy. In 1913, She was given the honor of unveiling the Seagull Monument on Temple Square. In 1914, a weary Emmeline relinquished control of the *Woman's Exponent*. The pioneering publication was to be superseded in 1916 by the *Relief Society Magazine*.

In 1914 a war broke out in Europe, a war that escalated to so many countries that it was called the "World War," or "the war to end all wars." In 1917, the United States was also pulled into the World War. The effects were devastating. Widespread starvation and disease covered Europe. The U.S. economy was still greatly dependent on agriculture. With man-power diverted to the war and war-related industries, the price of grain became grossly inflated, making wealthy those few with the foresight to hoard foodstuffs.

Almost ninety years of age, Emmeline watched the worsening war situation. Four decades before, Brigham Young had entrusted to Emmeline's direction the call to save grain and he prophesied there would come a time to use it. Emmeline had been faithful to that trust. She knew the time had come. The Relief Society would make a difference.

After negotiations with the United States, over two hundred thousand bushels of Relief Society wheat was sold to the U.S. government at a nominal deflated price. In remembrance, the Relief Society emblem carries the symbol of wheat, even today.

In 1919, at the age of ninety-one, Emmeline was bedridden with illness. A train pulled into Salt Lake City carrying dignitaries and bedecked with banners. The President of the United States, President Woodrow Wilson, and his wife, alit from the train. They went to Emmeline's apartment and were granted an audience with her. President Wilson sat by her sickbed and took her hand in his. He thanked Emmeline and the Relief Society, on behalf of the nation, for what they had done.

In Washington, D.C., the labors and sacrifice of the Relief Society had considerable impact, not only for the life-saving wheat but for the train-car loads of quilts, tens of thousands of knitted socks, bandages and other necessary supplies contributed to the war effort. In a government that had itself persecuted Mormons and challenged the loyalty of the Church, attitudes changed.

In 1921, at the age of ninety-three, Emmeline's health failed. She sent word to the current president of the Mormon Church, President Heber J. Grant, that it was time to release her from the presidency of the Relief Society. She was released and weeks later the tiny, quaint, romantic Emmeline Blanche Woodward Harris Whitney Wells passed away.

Emmeline's funeral was held in the Salt Lake Tabernacle, only the second woman to be so honored. Crowds filled the Tabernacle as dignitaries, church leaders and ordinary citizens alike came to honor Emmeline Wells. She died loved by thousands.

In 1928, on the 100th anniversary of Emmeline's birth, a marble bust of her was commissioned and placed in the State Capitol rotunda.

Emmeline's life had bridged two centuries. She had known the Prophet Joseph Smith and had lived to see the terms of six other presidents of the Church. She was born in an era when women were legally considered property instead of people, and she lived to see the empowerment of women prophesied by Joseph Smith. In her youth she experienced the migration of the Mormon pioneers and saw the building of great temples. She witnessed the pioneer struggles for primitive survival, and also lived to see a new century with electricity, telephones and automobiles. She had known and met with eleven presidents or former presidents of the United States of America and she had influenced legislation. Emmeline had been a part of it all, one of the influential women of her era.

Emmeline often pondered on life in her diary. In advanced age when she was finally courted by Daniel, she wrote, " . . . only memories, only the coming and going and parting at the door, the joy when he came, the sorrow when he went, as though all the light died out of my life. Such intense love he has manifested towards me of late years. Such a remarkable change from the long ago, when I needed him so much more, how peculiarly these things come about."

How strangely things do come about.

Ghost in the Picture

In the collection of the LDS Museum of Church History and Art in Salt Lake City there is a certain painting done by an artist named William Warner Major. You can also find a copy of the painting in the collections of the Utah State Historical Society. The painting shows a handsome pioneer family of the 1840s, dressed in Sunday best. The family portrait was painted in Nauvoo. It is a typical family painting of that era, except for one thing. If you had been there watching the family members being painted you would have seen seven family members posing. Yet there are eight people in the picture.

When Mary Ann Angell first heard young missionaries preach, she decided to move to New York to learn more of this new religion nicknamed "Mormonism." From New York she moved to Ohio. In a meeting there she bore testimony of the truth she heard. One young man, a missionary by the name of Brigham Young, was impressed by her. She was impressed by him. Brigham and Mary Ann married in February, 1834.

Mary Ann bore five children. In 1841, Brigham Young was out on another mission. Mary Ann wrote to her husband about their oldest daughter, also called Mary Ann, who was four years old. At night the little girl would refuse to go to bed till she got on her knees and prayed for her daddy in the mission field. This wrenched Brigham's heart and, although he longed to come home, he was committed to remain far away on an important mission.

Finally in 1843, when little Mary Ann was six years old, Mother had to write a heart-wrenching letter to Brigham. Little Mary Ann had taken ill and died. The little girl who would not go to bed without praying for her daddy was gone.

When Brigham came home, there was no little Mary Ann to greet him. Though the other children had also been ill, they survived, but not little Mary Ann. In 1844, mother Mary Ann Angell Young added to the family another member, a son.

The Nauvoo painting is one of the best-known and earliest-known likenesses of Brigham Young. As one looks at the family painting, painted when Brigham's youngest son was an infant, one can see the father seated on one side of the room, the mother on the other—their children between them. Next to Brigham stands son Joseph A. At his knee is daughter Luna. Standing next is Brigham, Jr. On the other side of the painting sits Mary Ann Young. On her lap is little John W. and by her knee is the family dog and little daughter Alice. In the center of the painting, in the middle of the family, is little Mary Ann. Little Mary Ann would have been eight if she had lived. The artist painted her as she would have looked.

Little Mary Ann was dead, but Brigham Young believed that in the eternities, she was still his little daughter, still a member of the family, and that she was still praying for him. She was painted in.

The years have passed. All in that family picture have passed on to join their heavenly families. Now, every person in the picture is just an image of someone who was once here, on this earth, for a short time.

Heavenly First Aid

T he history of first aid and of artificial respiration has changed over the centuries. For example, in centuries gone by, people of seafaring nations would roll a drowning victim over a barrel to force the water out and the air in.

In our own century artificial respiration was accomplished by a variety of procedures for pressing the chest and manipulating the body, often to the chant of "out with the bad air, in with the good." Books on first aid were published and distributed by the Red Cross. Courses were taught by the Red Cross throughout the world. In the late 1950's a technique of artificial respiration was developed that was superior to other techniques. It was "mouth-to-mouth resuscitation." Impressed by the importance of this discovery, the Red Cross in 1959 printed a fourteen-page pamphlet to supplement its previously published first aid books. The pamphlet announced,

> The National Academy of Sciences—National Research Council Ad Hoc Committee on Artificial Respiration in its meeting of 3 November 1958 reviewed the data on artificial respiration obtained through research projects supported by the Department of the Army, the American National Red Cross and others.
>
> It was unanimously agreed by members of the Ad Hoc group that the mouth-to-mouth (or mouth-to-nose) technique of artificial respiration is the most practical method for emergency ventilation of an individual of any age who has stopped breathing, in the absence of equipment or of help from a second person, regardless of the cause of cessation of breathing.

Thereafter, the pamphlet gave illustrated instructions for the technique.

Finally, in the 1960's, the mouth-to-mouth method of artificial respiration was introduced into newly published Red Cross first aid books.

In November of 1842, a pioneer family who had been driven from Missouri, losing nearly everything they had, were living in a roughly constructed cabin in Nauvoo. The cabin sat on low ground where frigid moisture seeped in. There was no door, only a blanket over the doorway. There was little food and no medical supplies. The pioneer father had been ill for days. His wife tended him as best she could with what they had. The man's condition only worsened.

On the eighteenth day of the illness, the man felt life leaving him. He felt so far gone that he could not close his eyes. His chin dropped to his chest. He ceased breathing.

The wife tried frantically to revive her husband. She threw cold water in his face. It had no effect. She had a handful of strong camphor which she dashed into his face and eyes. It had no effect. She was on the point of losing her husband when somehow she was guided. She knew what to do. She leaned over her husband, held his nostrils, placed her mouth directly over his and blew into his lungs until they were filled with air. She breathed for her husband till he was able to breathe again on his own.

The pioneer survived and recorded in his journal a small though amazingly detailed account of what his wife had done—more than a century before this method of resuscitation was known. The entry is dated November 26, 1842, an entry easily overlooked when you consider how much more he was to write. His writings and speeches would some day fill volumes. And volumes would be written about him—pioneer, empire builder, president and prophet of The Church of Jesus Christ of Latter-day Saints. Yet that small entry is one of the first recorded instances of mouth-to-mouth resuscitation: the cold day when Mary Ann Angell Young bent over and gave the breath of life to her husband, Brigham Young.

The Naughty Boy

When he was thirteen years old, George dropped out of school. The pleadings of his parents did no good. George was a willful boy. He wanted to do what he wanted to do.

George's gentle mother was not good at discipline. George's father was a generous man who gave money to anyone needing it, leaving his own family short. So George's mother created a secret emergency savings account, unknown to the rest of the family. Only George was taken into her confidence. Anytime George's mother saved a little money from the household budget, she had George slip over to the bank to deposit it.

Once, when George's mother tried to punish George for an infraction, George blackmailed her. He threatened to tell about the secret savings account. Mother backed down. George felt he could get away with anything. He continued to use this blackmail every time his mother tried to discipline him.

One day Mother had had enough. She punished George in spite of the blackmail. George, to his credit, did not give away the secret. Then soft-hearted Mother felt so bad for punishing her son that afterwards she bought George a hat that he wanted and that was the latest fad.

George's family moved to another city. That is when George's life changed. When he first entered the city, he saw a man standing in the middle of a crowd. Nobody pointed out the man to George and there was nothing in the crowd that separated the man from the others, but George knew—at first sight—that the man was a prophet. From that first sight, George's faith never wavered.

The new city was Nauvoo. The man George had seen in the crowd was Joseph Smith. Mother's secret bank account had helped pay for the family's ship passage across the sea.

The boy who dropped out of school became one of the most learned men of his time. And George Q. Cannon, the naughty boy, became an apostle and counselor to prophets Brigham Young, John Taylor, Wilford Woodruff and Lorenzo Snow.

Maori Prophecy

A mong the Maori people of New Zealand there were many sages believed to have the gift of prophecy. Several prophecies were made that seemed to foretell the coming of The Church of Jesus Christ of Latter-day Saints. This is the story of one of those prophecies.

In 1881, a convention was held for the representatives and natives of the Ngatikahungunu Tribe. At the convention, leaders of the Ngatikahungunus discussed the problems that were important to their people. One of those problems was how to know which church was right. Many were persuaded by Christianity, and many Christian religions had sent their missionaries, but this caused confusion to the people.

The leaders discussed and debated this question at great length. Finally it was proposed that the question be addressed to the wisest and most learned of the chiefs, Paora Potangaroa. Paora Potangaroa retired from the people and was for three days occupied in meditation, fasting and prayer. After three days he returned to the convention. He said to the people, "The church for the Maori people has not yet come among us. You will recognize it when it comes. Its missionaries will travel in pairs. They will come from the rising sun (east). They will visit with us in our homes. They will learn our language and teach us the gospel in our own tongue. When they pray they will raise their right hands."

Before Paora Potangaroa continued his prophecy, a scribe was called to record it. The scribe was named Ranginui Kingi. Chief Potangaroa continued his prophecy naming years when the things he prophesied would come to pass, beginning with the first year, that very year, when the true gospel would come, followed by years when they would learn gospel principles and receive sealing ordinances.

He named many other details, such as that the people shall be taught they are lost sheep of the house of Israel, that the missionaries would come from across the ocean and that they would come from "the sacred Church with a large wall surrounding." A drawing of the "all-seeing eye" was drawn on the document. The document was dated March 16, 1881.

To commemorate Potangaroa's prophecy and the writing of it, a cement monument was erected at the historic meeting house where the convention was held. The document was placed in the monument.

That year, just as Potangaroa had prophesied, the first of the Latter-day Saint missionaries to the Maori people, Elder W. M. Bromley of Springville, Utah, arrived among the Maori people. Great numbers of the Ngatikahungunu tribe and other Maori people joined the Church.

In 1929, members of a group called the Ratana Church broke apart the cement monument to obtain the recorded prophecy, hoping they would find it to apply to themselves. The prophecy had not been hermetically sealed and the paper had, as a result, disintegrated. It was gone.

In 1944, Matthew Cowley was presiding over the New Zealand Mission. He attended a conference of the Church in the Ngatikahungunu region. At the conference, an elderly member of the church, Brother Eriata Nopera, told of his being present, as a youth, at the convention of the leaders of the Ngatikahungunu Tribe in 1881. He told of hearing the prophecies of Potangaroa foretelling the coming of the Church to the Maori people. At the end of the meeting, a Maori sister told her husband to go to their house quickly and bring back a package in brown paper from the bottom of her trunk. The husband returned and his wife unrolled the brown wrapping paper, presenting the contents to Brother Nopera.

It seems that at the time of the convention in 1881, there was a photographer living in the nearby town of Masterton. Having heard of the prophecy, the photographer had asked permission to come and photograph it. Permission was granted.

It was this photograph, sixty years old, preserved and passed down through a Maori family as a sacred possession, that was presented to Brother Nopera, who turned it over to President Cowley. Long thought lost, the document was preserved as a testimony for today.

Test of Brotherhood

W ith the coming of the twentieth century, The Church of Jesus Christ of Latter-day Saints has reached out to all the corners of the world. Yet, sometimes the brotherhood of the gospel is tested by cultural, social and ethnic differences.

In August 1941, President David O. McKay visited Hawaii. Conferences were held. The Saints he visited came from a colorful variety of backgrounds. Members of the Japanese Mission in Hawaii held the first session of the conference in the new tabernacle in Honolulu. The all-Japanese choir sang, "We Thank Thee, O God, for a Prophet," in the Japanese language.

Among the speakers at the Japanese conference was a youth speaker named Yoshio. He was a new member of the Church. Yoshio's family had come from Hiroshima, Japan, to find work in Hawaii. His family was Buddhist. Some friends of his played basketball with missionaries from a Christian church. He was invited to play with them. He began attending M.I.A. He began learning about the gospel. After two years, he desired to join the Church and was the only member of his family to do so. It was at this conference attended by the President of the Church that he was honored to speak about opportunities for youth in the Church.

At the conclusion of the conference session, President McKay compared the nationalities and races who made up the congregation to a 'harmony of colors.' He said that the barriers that exist in the minds of some are overcome by the love of Christ and the acceptance of the gospel. He quoted Paul in Galatians: "There is neither Jew nor Greek, there is neither bond nor free, there is neither male nor female: for ye are all one in Christ Jesus."

In less than four months, the brotherhood of which President McKay spoke was put to the test. In December came the bombing of

Pearl Harbor. The love of many good members was not affected by the trying times. But suspicion, bias and furor affected others in their feelings toward other Church members. The Japanese Saints felt ostracized by many.

Young Yoshio had dreamed of going on a mission for the Church. On the day he was to go he was instead drafted into the U.S. Army's 441st Counterintelligence Corps. He was separated from his family and from his Church. But the Church did not forget young Yoshio. He was to help bring again that 'harmony of colors.'

In 1965, Yoshio was called as mission president of the Northern Far East Mission. In 1970, he was named Regional Representative over Japan and Hawaii. By then he had long discontinued using the name 'Yoshio' because of confusion with another person who bore the same name.

In 1975, he was sustained a general authority, the first general authority of Japanese descent. Finally, in 1993, at the age seventy, after nearly a lifetime of service to the Church, emeritus status was given to Elder Adney Y. Komatsu.

Japanese Land

In 1948, after World War II, Edward L. Clissold was sent to Japan to reopen the LDS mission there. His first task was to find housing for the missionaries that would follow. Because of the bombings and property confiscations during the war, very little land or housing was available to anyone, let alone a foreign mission president.

Miraculously, through the assistance of new friends, President Clissold was introduced to the business advisor of Prince Takamatsu. The advisor, Mr. Kawasoe, recommended two properties—both bombed and totally gutted. President Clissold became interested in one of the properties, the one in Azabu which had been the residence of the former Minister of Welfare of the Japanese government. It was gutted, bombed and had no roof, but much of it was still structurally sound. The location was good. It was near embassies and a park and was five minutes from downtown Tokyo. President Clissold received permission from the Church for the purchase. After cutting through much local red tape, the property was purchased for $10,000. Reconstruction began and the mission home was built on that site.

President Clissold was soon followed by the first five missionaries to enter Japan after the war. All five had done service fighting Japan during the war. All five had difficult feelings to overcome, but they quickly learned to love the people they had so recently fought. Their first task was to find the Japanese people who had been members before the war.

The mission in Japan had not been productive prior to World War II, yielding less than 200 members. As the missionaries sought for the original members, they found some in shacks and lean-tos, their homes destroyed, yet shedding tears of joy that the Church had found them.

In 1949, Elder Matthew Cowley of the Council of Twelve traveled to Japan to the new mission home. He offered the dedicatory prayer and uttered a prophecy that in this land would be built many churches and temples.

Though the thought of a temple in Japan seemed remote in that place with less than 200 members, Elder Cowley's prophecy came to pass. In 1975, President Spencer W. Kimball announced the plans for the Tokyo Temple. It was completed in 1980. One of the five missionaries who had been present at the prophecy of Elder Cowley was Elder Harrison Ted Price. He returned to Japan as mission president in 1976. Not only did he see the prophecy come to pass, he watched the temple being constructed on the very spot where the prophecy had been made. The temple was built on the location of the mission home.

At the reopening of the mission in 1948, the missionaries found the Japanese people much more open to the gospel. Part of this was because of the missionary labors of LDS servicemen who had been in the occupation forces. The Church found open doors and welcome hearts.

President Clissold and Elder Cowley traveled through Japan looking for possible sites for chapels. In the city of Shibata, they were welcomed by the mayor who not only gave them a place to meet but sent one hundred and six of the city's leading businessmen and civic leaders to listen to them. One of the wealthy men of the city was Mr. Ichishima. He had been the second-largest landowner in Japan prior to the war. Though his holdings were reduced, they were still considerable. Mr. Ichishima offered the Church an estate in Tennen Shinden consisting of several buildings and seventeen hundred acres. Elder Cowley said he would have to have permission from the Church authorities to accept such a gift. He received the permission. Missionaries were sent. Two weeks later, when Elder Cowley visited the estate, he found a congregation of two hundred and fourteen people worshiping there with Mr. Ichishima playing the organ for them.

Elder Cowley asked Mr. Ichishima why he made this great offer to the Mormons. Mr. Ichishima said, "There is a man here named Mr. Mogi, and Mr. Mogi told me to give it to the Mormons. Many years ago he used to live in Mexico among Mormon people. He said, 'I saw what those people can do, their spirit of cooperation, the way they lived; good, clean living, good habits and morals—that has remained with me all the days of my life. And so I said, let's find the Mormons.'"

Seventeen hundred acres and several beautiful buildings were given to help build the Church in Japan. It cost the Church nothing, all because a man lived among the Mormons in Mexico and was inspired in a way that affected his life.

That is how the love of the Saints in Mexico provided land for the Church in Japan.

Taters and Testimony

The woman believed she was dying. She said she was dying, though the doctor found nothing wrong with her. The woman had one last request—that someone sing her a hymn. No one would volunteer to sing the woman a hymn. They'd been through this before. Finally, the doctor volunteered to sing a hymn. To the tune of "Camptown Races" he sang out:

A jay bird a settin' on a hickory limb,
Doo dah, Doo dah
He winked at me and I winked at him,
Doo dah Doo dah day."

The dying woman arose in anger and indignation, completely forgetting that she thought she was going to die. The doctor was a humorous but practical man with little time to waste.

Dr. Anderson Grigg and his wife Casadria were of Quaker stock. They lived in the rugged woods of North Carolina. Though some of the doctor's patients were well-to-do, most were poor people from the back woods.

In 1839, the Grigg family first heard the gospel. When persecution began, they still stayed loyal to their beliefs. Along with their loyalty to the Church, the Grigg family had strong political opinions. They were anti-slavery. In 1846, Dr. Grigg's father, Billy Grigg, was murdered by neighbors at the polls when he went to vote.

Dr. Grigg knew of Joseph Smith's prophecy of the Civil War (Doctrine and Covenants Section 87) and was there thirty years later to see the fulfillment. Although living in the South, Dr. Grigg's son William joined the Union forces. His son James joined the Confederate forces. His son Parley wanted to join the Union forces, but he was still a boy so Dr. Grigg would not allow him. Still,

Parley had to be hidden from the Rebel Homeguard or he would be shot on sight.

All during the war and for a few years after, the Grigg family had no word of the Church. They had heard about the Church moving west but did not know what had become of it. One day Dr. Grigg saw a newspaper article saying that Brigham Young and the Church were getting the contract to furnish ties to the Union Pacific railroad going west. Dr. Grigg wrote to the Church in Utah and the family soon immigrated.

Dr. Grigg had a son, Parley, who was named for his favorite missionary, Parley P. Pratt. Little did Dr. Grigg know at the time that his son Parley would have a son named Parley, Jr. and that Parley Jr. would marry the granddaughter of Parley P. Pratt. Parley Jr. and his wife Thankful had several children, including two sons named Golden and Nephi.

One cold and windy day when they were in their late teens, Golden and Nephi were plowing a field in Idaho and talking about how much of the world they hadn't seen. They made a sudden decision. Stopping where they were, they unhitched the horses from the plow. They took off their bridles and collars and turned the horses loose. Golden and Nephi hitchhiked through the Western States.

In 1934, Golden and Nephi started growing and marketing sweet corn. They formed the Grigg Brothers Produce Company. In 1949 they experimented with freezing the corn and potatoes. They obtained patents for processing and freezing raw, shoe string, hashed brown, mashed and baked potatoes. They continued to experiment and expand. Their business prospered.

Along with business responsibilities, they served the Church in a number of callings. One time, after being called to be a bishop, Nephi was talking with a Protestant minister. The minister asked how much Nephi was paid to be a bishop. Nephi explained that bishops don't get paid. On the contrary, they pay ten percent of their income in tithing. Nephi asked the minister how much he was paid.

The minister stated his salary. Nephi laughed and said he paid more than that to the Church as tithing. Nephi went on to serve as mission president in Scotland and was awarded the Silver Beaver and the Silver Antelope for his participation in Boy Scouting.

Throughout their lives, the Grigg brothers represented the Church well in their business and civic duties.

Today, Golden and Nephi Grigg are known as the founders of Ore-Ida Foods, inventors of the Tater-Tot. After Ore-Ida was sold to the H. J. Heinz Company, Nephi served for a while as the director of that Company.

That is how a family that started with a testimony in the back woods of North Carolina became developers of a brand name known in every household today.

Attack of the Dead Cat

Parowan is southern Utah's oldest permanent settlement. It was settled by pioneers in 1851 and was named the county seat of Iron County.

Among the early settlers of Parowan was the Marsden family. Their son, Lucius, was born there. When Lucius was about ten, he and two other boys, William Thornton and Frank Orton, got into mischief. There was an old log school house in Parowan. Like the school houses of that time, it was one big room with a large, round stove in the middle to keep it warm on cold days or cold nights, as the case may be. The school house had windows on the east and west, with a door on the south. Lucius and his friends knew that the young men in the community would sneak over to the school house at night, warm up the stove, and engage in the questionable activity of "card playing."

Aware of the sneakiness of the big boys of the community, the three young boys decided to engage in some sneakiness of their own. Lucius knew where there was a cat. The cat was big and, most importantly, the cat was dead. Lucius led the other two boys behind the Court House where they found the cat frozen stiff. They got the cat and took it over to the school house. While the young men inside were raucously enjoying their card game, Lucius and his friends slowly raised the window. William held the window up so that Frank could throw the cat through. Frank was left-handed and had to make several swings before he could get the dead cat through the window. The swings of the corpse got a little too close to William's head and William, fearing he would be hit, dropped the window at the exact moment that Frank let go of the cat. The stiff cat crashed through the window, breaking sash and all, and landed in the middle of the card players. The card players, not knowing what desperate beast had attacked, scattered like the wind. They ran out of the school as fast as they could go. The three boys, equally frightened, ran as fast as they could go in the other direction.

When the school trustees found out who broke the window, the three boys were forced to repair it. William and Frank made a new sash and Lucius filled it with glass.

The "Attack of the Dead Cat" eventually faded to memory. Lucius Marsden grew up to commit his creative talents to other pursuits. He became president of the Bank of Iron County, councilman and Mayor of Parowan, a Utah State senator, and President of the Parowan Stake.

Tale of the Buckskin Pants

In 1861 the Overland Telegraph, approaching simultaneously from east and west, met in Salt Lake City, linking a continent with lines of communication. The first message sent out from Salt Lake City was from Brigham Young. "Utah has not seceded," telegraphed Young, "but is firm for the Constitution and laws of our once happy country . . . ."

The acting governor of the Utah Territory, Frank Fuller, followed up the message with one to President Lincoln. He telegraphed, "Utah, whose citizens strenuously resist all imputations of disloyalty, congratulates the President upon the completion of an enterprise which spans a continent, unites two oceans, and connects with nerve of iron the remote extremities of the body politic with the great governmental heart."

President Lincoln answered back, "The completion of the telegraph to Great Salt Lake City is auspicious of the stability and union of the republic."

These messages were significant for two reasons. First was the question of Utah loyalty. Less than five years earlier, under President Buchanan, an army had been sent to Utah because of false rumors of rebellion. Second, the nation itself had just separated in Civil War. The message let President Lincoln know that Utah was for the preserved union of the United States.

President Lincoln acted on that declaration of loyalty. U.S. troops, recalled from the West to fight in the Civil War, needed replacements. In 1862, President Lincoln telegraphed Brigham Young asking for Utah troops to serve as guards for the overland telegraph, stage and mail routes. The necessary troops were mustered and put under the leadership of Lot Smith, the very man who had harassed and delayed the U.S. Army only a few years before. But Lot Smith knew the territory and his men were tested.

It was in this setting that the unusual episode of the buckskin pants occurred. Two members of the Lot Smith expedition during the Civil War period, "Shorty" and "Slim," were both in need of pants. Their homespun pants were greatly worn. Word reached camp that an Indian squaw was making a pair of buckskin pants for her brave. Shorty and Slim visited the squaw in an effort to persuade her to sell the pants. Shorty offered her a $5 gold piece. The squaw thought it looked small and would not trade. Slim had a bright idea and offered the squaw $5 worth of silver half-dollars and quarters. To the squaw it appeared as much more money, so she sold Slim the pants.

Early next morning, the company set off in pursuit of a band of raiding Indians. Slim rode proudly in his new buckskins and was the envy of the camp. Crossing the Snake River, the pants became soaked, and as buckskin does, began to lengthen and stretch till it interfered with the use of Slim's stirrups. Not knowing the consequences, Slim reached for his pocket knife and slashed off the bottoms of the pants.

As the hot afternoon wore on, the buckskin pants began to dry and simultaneously to shrink. When the company finally halted to encamp for the night, Slim's pants had halted just above the knees. The camp, infested with mosquitoes, increased Slim's discomfort. Previous envious glances from Slim's comrades were exchanged for laughter and jests.

Early next morning, Slim surveyed the remainder of his pants and angrily threw them over the limb of a tree. A companion gave him a discarded pair of homespun pants that were worse than the homespuns he started with, yet provided him some covering.

That night Slim was captured by the Indians and after two days' imprisonment, was brought before Washakie, chief of the Shoshones, fearing and trembling. Washakie asked, "You Mormon?"

Slim answered, "Yes."

"You after Indians!"

Here Slim saw a glimmer of light and gained courage. "Oh no, we don't want to hurt the Indians, but Washakie, you must leave the mail and stage line alone. There is a wagon load of presents at Fort Bridger sent for you by Brigham Young. If you will pilot me safely back there, I will see to it that you receive these wonderful presents." And he gave silent thanks to Brigham Young's diplomacy and his policy to "feed them, don't fight them."

Washakie's face beamed with delight and he extended Slim a cordial invitation to dine at his neighbor's, a brave named Rain-in-the-Face.

Slim soon found himself seated in the wickiup of Rain-in-the-Face, holding in his hand a steaming bowl of soup. The broth tasted queer, but as he had not eaten for two days, he readily gulped it down. Upon rising to leave, he wished to please his host by complimenting him. So he told him how much he had enjoyed the soup and wondered what it could be made of.

Rain-in-the-Face explained how his eldest son, Wampu, two days previously, had discovered a piece of rawhide hanging over the limb of a tree. From this rawhide they had made the "soup."

Escape from Liberty

Most students of the history of The Church of Jesus Christ of Latter-day Saints are familiar with the incarceration of Joseph Smith and his companions at Liberty Jail, which led to the revelations found in Doctrine and Covenants sections 121, 122 and 123. Not as many are familiar with the "escape" from Liberty Jail.

Missouri in the 1830s was the rough, sometimes lawless, frontier of the new country of the United States. There was great religious fervor and great political fervor as well. Slavery was a hotly debated issue that was popular in Missouri. The Mormons were essentially anti-slavers. Land was currently being wrested from the local Indians, but the Mormons were preaching to the Indians and trying to convert them. The Mormons lived in closed communities, causing suspicion by others.

Some of the older settlers of Missouri welcomed the civilizing influence of the Mormons. Others older settlers were frightened by the unchecked flow of immigrants into their area. In two years alone over a thousand Mormons bought and settled land, causing some of the older settlers to fear political and economic domination by a strange sect.

These were some of the causes that led to mob violence against the Saints in the rough, frontier times of Missouri. Ruffians at the voting polls violently denied Mormons the vote. Vigilante groups raided Mormon settlements, attacking, beating, burning, looting, murdering. The Mormons appealed to the courts, to no avail.

Major General David R. Atchinson tried to protect Mormon settlements with state militia but was undermined by mutiny and insubordination. Mormons organized to protect their interests and this organization was perceived and reported as aggression.

In 1838, acting on the reported abductions of two Saints, a posse of Mormons aggressively pursued a mob of renegade Missouri militia to Crooked Creek. A battle occurred there costing the lives of one mobocrat and three Mormons. News of the Mormon "aggression" was taken straightway to Governor Lilburn Boggs who issued his infamous "Extermination Order." Now Mormons could "legally" be killed or driven from the state because of their religious affiliation.

With the law on their side the mobocrats murdered, looted and confiscated lands, homes, stock and possessions of the Saints. Appeals to the courts went unanswered. Joseph Smith, Hyrum Smith, Lyman Wight and others went to resolve the dispute and were arrested by Major General Samuel D. Lucas, himself one of the purveyors of false rumors. He ordered the prisoners to be shot without a valid trial. Brigadier General Alexander Doniphan refused the order and promised to bring to justice anyone who tried to execute the captives. The prisoners were then sent to Liberty Jail where they were held, without a valid trial or due process of law, in horrible conditions for several months.

The Missouri Legislature met in session in 1839 to debate the legality of Governor Boggs "executive order." It was supported by citizens of northwestern Missouri but was warmly denounced by others. The debate dragged on till the point was moot, for the Saints had been driven from the State.

After months of illegal incarceration in Liberty jail, Joseph Smith and his fellow prisoners escaped — with the help of those who had held them prisoners but knew they were being illegally detained. Because of mob rule in the area, the judge, sheriff and guards, at great risk to themselves, secretly plotted the escape. According to an affidavit of Hyrum Smith given July 1, 1843, the prisoners were ordered to be removed to Boone County. While they were being transported and were nearly there, "the sheriff showed us the mittimus before referred to, without date or signature, and said that Judge Birch told him never to carry us to Boone County, and never to show the mittimus; and, said he, I shall take a good drink of grog, and go to bed, and you may do as you have a mind to." The prisoners, having a mind to leave, did so after the sheriff and guards were asleep; except for one guard who helped saddle the two horses the prisoners had between them. The prisoners fled and made their way east to Nauvoo, Illinois where they rejoined their families and the rest of the Saints.

One of the strangest things about this story is what happened a century later. In 1976, it was discovered that the "Extermination Order" was still on the books, and it was still "legal" in the state of Missouri to kill a Mormon because of his religious affiliation. Governor Christopher S. Bond, the Governor of the State of Missouri, at that time, quickly remedied the embarrassing oversight. In an executive order dated June 25, 1976, Governor Bond rescinded the "Extermination Order" and formally apologized to The Church of Jesus Christ of Latter-day Saints on behalf of the State of Missouri—one hundred and thirty-eight years after the cruel and infamous order was first issued.

No Place to Lose a Cow

When the Mormons settled Utah, they set out to carve a place for themselves in the wilderness. Unfortunately, the wilderness was often a hostile and difficult thing to tame. The Saints endured great hardships and sufferings. To lighten their loads they enjoyed dance, storytelling and humor. Southern Utah, also known as Utah's Dixie, was especially inhospitable. At a concert in 1870 in St. George, Brigham Young and George A. Smith (for whom the town was named) were present when Charles Walker, the leading poet of Southern Utah, presented his newest song. It was called, "Saint George and the Drag-On:"

> Oh, what a desert place was this
> When first the Mormons found it;
> They said no white man here could live
> And the Indians prowl'd around it.
> They said the land it was no good,
> And the water was no gooder,
> And the bare idea of living here
> Was enough to make one shudder.

(Chorus)

> Mesquite, soap root, prickly-pears and briars,
> St. George ere long will be a place
>   that everyone admires."

Said one pioneer living in St. George, "Well, when I die I can go either of two ways. I can go to heaven or I can be sent back here." Pioneers would jest that it was so much like hell that even the toads wore horns. It was so hot that chickens laid eggs fried. The wind blew so hard that when they planted a seed, they had to hold it down

with a foot till it grew. In his journal in 1861, Robert Gardner recorded his reaction after being called to settle Southern Utah. "I looked
and spit, took off my hat and scratched my head and said all right."

One adventurous traveler, on visiting Southern Utah and seeing
the colorful wilderness, said, "It looks like Hell." "My," answered a
local citizen, "you've been everywhere."

There's the story of another visitor to Utah's Dixie who made
the mistake of asking, "Does it ever rain here?" The resident
answered, "Remember when Noah built the ark and it rained
forty days and forty nights? We got an inch and a half then."

Bryce Canyon, a national park since 1923, is world renowned for
its vividly colored sandstone formations and canyons sculpted by
erosion. The canyon is named for Mormon pioneer Ebeneezer Bryce
who called it "A hell of a place to lose a cow."

Utah's Dixie became known for characters just as colorful as the
local canyons. One of these was Bill Braxton. It is said that a Brother
Warren was once Bill's "ward" or "home" teacher. Many of the early
pioneers had problems with the Word of Wisdom, including Bill. So
Brother Warren delivered Bill a sermon on improving his life. After
the visit, Bill escorted Brother Warren to the door and said, "Well, I
smoke and you steal chickens so I guess we'll reach heaven about the
same time."

Another time Bill said there were three liars in Washington
County. He was one and Henry Holt was the other two. When one of
Bill's daughters went with a young man that Bill didn't like, Bill met
him when he came to call. Said Bill, "If you come back here again,
I'll kick you so far that your clothes will be old fashioned when you
get back."

The pioneers had to be tough. Little food would grow. The elements were harsh. Diseases like typhoid took their toll, especially of
the children. Still, the pioneers did the best they could with what they
had. In 1875, the citizens celebrated Independence Day. Charles
Walker provided this entertaining song:

At sunrise Bands of Music played
Sweet strains they did discourse.
The Procession tramped around the town
With the Mayor upon a horse.
The Procession to the Bowery went.
No Declaration read.
There would have been some toast that day
But the folks were short of Bread.
'Tis the driest fourth we ever saw.
No Meat or cheese to buy.
And all the fun the citizens had,
You could stick it in your eye.
A sumptuous feast was then prepared,
Description it surpasses,
Consisting of some caneseed bread
Served up with burnt Molasses.
Some soap root beer was passed around
Sour enough to make you cry
And all the fun the citizens had
You could stick it in your eye.
May such a dry old stupid fourth
St. George ne'er see again.
It was so hot the clouds took fire
And burnt up all the rain.
Our fame has spread clear from St. Joe's
To Bear Lake in the north
Of the Great big thundering *spludge* we had
In St. George upon the fourth.

He Spoke with Humor and Persuasive Power

"I'm no speaker," said John Taylor. "You don't have to tell the people that for they've already found out . . . ."

John Taylor, however, was a gifted speaker. He served missions to Canada, England and France. His writings and speeches converted thousands.

Taylor survived great persecutions in the early days of the Church. He lost homes and property. He was seriously injured at the attack on Carthage Jail.

After migrating west, he had little patience when persecutions followed the Church. "They want a cause to quarrel . . . don't give it to them," said Taylor of government officials sent to Utah to quash Mormonism. "They are bent on provoking a quarrel and mischief . . . it takes two to make a quarrel, don't you be one of them . . . they offer themselves to be kicked. Don't do it, have some respect for your boots."

Again he said, "Minie rifles, Colt's revolvers, sabers and cannon may display very good workmanship and great artistic skill, but we very much object to having their temper and capabilities tried upon us . . . The guillotine may be a very pretty instrument and show great artistic skill, but I don't like to try my neck in it." Later he exclaimed, "What! Won't you submit to the dignity of the law? Well, I would if the law would only be a little more dignified."

In a Sunday morning meeting after arriving in the Salt Lake Valley, John Taylor asked, in a sermon, "What was your object in coming here? Was it to rebel against the general government?"

Sitting behind him, Brigham Young spoke out, "To get away from Christians," and the congregation exploded with laughter.

Speaking of the persecutors, Taylor time and again quoted two of his favorite sayings: "We came West to the deserts of Utah willingly because we had to," and, "Remember the Mormon Creed: Mind your own business and let everybody else do likewise."

Taylor carried his sense of humor into his personal life. He wrote of an incident in Nauvoo. He told how he had kissed his family goodbye and was about to depart, and then he wrote, "I went to a house adjoining the river, owned by Brother Eddy. There I disguised myself so as not to be known, and so effectually was the transformation that those who had come after me with a boat did not know me. I went down to the boat and sat in it. Brother Bell, thinking I was a stranger, watched my moves for some time very impatiently, and then said to Brother Wheelock, 'I wish that old gentleman would go away; he has been puttering around the boat for some time, and I am afraid Elder Taylor will be coming.' When he discovered his mistake, he was not a little amused."

When a member of Brother Taylor's family was in dire financial circumstances, he sent his new overcoat to be sold saying, "I can get along very nicely with my old coat this winter. It is a little faded, but then I prefer a faded coat to a faded reputation."

Taylor used humor in his preaching. He cited a prayer to show his attitude toward selfishness:

> Lord, bless me and my wife,
> My son John and his wife,
> Us four, but no more. Amen.

He spoke of trying to get people to do what they didn't want to do: "A man said, 'I can call spirits from the vasty deep!' 'So can I,' shouted another, but they won't come.'"

John Taylor often spoke to people with beliefs other than his own. While preaching in Ohio, he demonstrated a masterly use of reverse psychology. He was staying in a town where several people were anxiously awaiting his speech. A little before the meeting, several of the brethren came running to tell him that the whole town was gathering. A mob was forming and several men were boasting that they would tar and feather Taylor if he tried to preach. The brethren fearfully advised Taylor not to go to the meeting. They knew the tar and feathers were already prepared. They urged him to escape.

Taylor thought about it, then said that he would go to the meeting and if they did not care to go, he would go alone.

At the meeting, a large crowd of people was gathered. Taylor began by saying that he had just come from Canada, a land under monarchical rule, and that standing as he was on free soil among free men, he experienced peculiar sensations. "Gentlemen, I now stand among men whose fathers fought for and obtained one of the greatest blessings ever conferred upon the human family—the right to think, to speak, to write; the right to say who shall govern them, and the right to worship God according to the dictates of their own consciences—all of them sacred, human rights, and now guaranteed by the American Constitution." Taylor began to compliment the crowd. "I see around me the sons of those noble sires, who, rather than bow to the behests of a tyrant, pledged their lives, fortunes and sacred honors to burst those fetters, enjoy freedom themselves, bequeath it to their posterity, or die in the attempt.

"They nobly fought and nobly conquered; and now the cap of liberty is elevated on the tops of your liberty poles throughout the land, and the flag of freedom waves from Wisconsin to Louisiana—from Maine to Missouri. Not only so, but your vessels—foremost in the world—sail over oceans, seas and bays; visiting every nation, and wherever those vessels go your flag flutters in the breeze, a hope is inspired among the down-trodden millions, that they, perchance, if they cannot find liberty in their own land, may find it with you." He continued to compliment them in a profuse and majestic manner. ". . . With you liberty is more than a name; it is incorporated in your system; it is proclaimed by your senators; thundered by your cannon; lisped by your infants; taught to your schoolboys; it echoes from mountain to mountain; reverberates through your valleys; and is whispered by every breeze. Is it any wonder, gentlemen, under these circumstances—having lately emerged from a monarchical government, that I should experience peculiar sensations in rising to address you?"

As no one moved to stop Taylor's complimentary speaking, he began to preach the gospel and continued for three hours. Afterwards he was greeted warmly by the leading citizens of the town, and when the subject of tar and feathering was mentioned, they denied that anything like that would happen there.

John Taylor served as third President of The Church of Jesus Christ of Latter-day Saints till his death in 1887.

J. Golden
and the Brass Band

One of the most beloved leaders of The Church of Jesus Christ of Latter-day Saints was J. Golden Kimball. He had a way of relating to the common man. "When I look over this body of men," he said in conference, "I do not discover that you are very distinguished in appearance. Why, you are no better looking than I am, and I look pretty bad. I am only a remnant of what I ought to be. I am not very well groomed, and I do not look distinguished; neither do you."

He was an odd figure with a high-pitched voice. One time he walked into a clothing store and said to the clerk, "I'd like to see a suit that will fit me." The clerk looked up and down the tall, skinny figure and replied, "So would I."

Golden was sometimes mystified by his calling to be a General Authority. He said that there were three ways to be called to that position—inspiration, revelation, or relation. He put himself in the third category. He often felt inadequate for such an august position and was open in expressing it. "We went on a six week's trip through the southern part of the state," he once told. "We held two or three meetings each day. At Kanab conference I listened to Brother Francis M. Lyman for a long time. Then I dozed off and had a dream. I dreamed I was falling over a cliff one hundred feet high. I wondered how long it would be before I hit the bottom. Finally I landed stretched out on the platform, helpless and discomfited before four hundred people. Brother Lyman turned and said, 'Young man, you have ruined one of my best sermons.' It cured me of sleeping in church."

He seemed always in awe that he was in a leadership position, as indicated by these quotes from conference talks over the years:

1904: "I am ready to confess that I am keyed up to a pretty high tension, and the only thing I am afraid of is that I will say just what I think, which would be unwise, no doubt."

1904: "When an apostate lifts up his voice against this people, when he makes dastardly charges against the Latter-day Saints, he lies, and I have no patience with him. I have breathed this mountain air so long that I feel inclined to discard a little of the Gospel and knock such men down, and repent afterwards."

1906: "I realize that my reputation of wisdom has been greatly injured by repeating jokes in my public utterances and that, because of my calling in the ministry, I should, in the estimation of some people, be as solemn as an owl. . . . It is considered a good thing to look wise, especially when not overburdened with information."

1907: "You know there is no other man like me in all Israel and probably you are glad of it. . . . If I can be saved it is an encouragement to every man, woman and child in Israel to make the effort."

1919: ". . . I love God . . . I know that He will deal justly with me; and the great joy I will have is that He will understand me, and that is more than some of you have been able to do."

1932: "Now, what I am trying to get at is this: it takes intelligent people to understand what I am trying to get at. . . . If I give you a little chaff to get you to take a little wheat, my trouble has always been, you choose the chaff and lose the wheat."

Though J. Golden's humor put people at ease, he was not always at ease himself. His own life had been one of trials, poverty, illness and hardship. In 1883, thirty-year-old J. Golden went to the Southern States mission. He traveled without purse or scrip, often hungry and sleeping on the hard ground. He was made mission secretary to the mission president, twenty-six-year-old B. H. Roberts. Missionaries in that era were mobbed, beaten, shot, driven out of towns. At a place called Kane Creek, a mob killed two missionaries and two other members. J. Golden was the first to get news of the massacre. He and President Roberts risked their lives to go into the area and retrieve the bodies of the missionaries. J. Golden later returned to the same mission as mission president. In the April, 1932 Conference, he told this story:

> When I was president of the Southern States Mission, after a year's time I concluded that I would try to hold a conference in a city.
>
> When we went to the court house...all those present were men. There wasn't a woman among them, and we all knew what that meant. When there are no women, there is a great deal of danger. . . . At any rate, I made up my mind to deliver my message as fervently and humbly as ever a president of a mission preached . . .
>
> I went there determined to preach the Gospel. I had my Bible, and I am well acquainted with my Bible. I cannot find anything in anybody else's Bible. . . . I went there believing that the Spirit of God was on me as the president of the mission . . .
>
> I got up to preach the Gospel, faith and repentance, etc. All at once something came over me and I opened my mouth and said to that body of men: (the building was crowded, among them were some of the leading men) 'Gentlemen, you have not come here to listen to the Gospel of Jesus Christ. I know what you have come for. You have come to find out about the Mountain Meadows Massacre and polygamy; and God, being my helper, I will tell you the truth.' And I did. I talked to them for one hour. (I said to those elders: 'Don't one of you dare preach that sermon; it will cost you your life.' And I have never preached it since.)
>
> When the meeting was out you could hear a pin drop. There was no comment; there was no noise or confusion, and we went to the hotel. We had arranged for lodgings at the cheap hotel. Soon we heard a band playing outside. Elder Willard Bean was the president of the conference. I sent him out to find what it all meant. I thought it meant trouble. So he inquired and they told him: 'We're serenading that big long fellow.' That is the only brass band I have ever had dispense music after one of my talks.

He Couldn't Be Broken

"Uncle Jesse" was a man some of the richest and most powerful men in the country tried to break but couldn't. He was born in Nauvoo and crossed the plains to Utah as a child. He grew up with the poverty and hardships of the pioneers. He got jobs in the mining camps and railroad camps of the West. He lost his testimony of the gospel.

Though he distanced himself from the Church, he married a good Mormon girl and had several children. One day a dead rat got in the family well. His five children became ill. Jesse began to reevaluate his life and his relationship with his Heavenly Father. Four of the children lived and one of the children died, but by then Jesse had regained his testimony, an incredible faith that would follow him throughout the rest of his life.

Utah was being discovered and exploited for its mining wealth. Because of Brigham Young's emphasis on settlement and farming, the mines were developed and capitalized by outside people. The Mormons saw none of the wealth. By the 1890's, Jesse thought it was time for the Mormons to gain from the local resources.

Jesse was not rich, yet he gave what he could to anyone who asked. He cosigned loans for people who cheated him. He learned a lot about trust, human nature and managing finances. One day he learned of a friend's intentions to cheat him in business. He went into the mountains to think. He was sitting under a pine tree when he heard a voice say to him, "This country is here for the Mormons." There was no one around, yet he had distinctly heard the voice and knew what it meant. He believed God was giving him a call and telling him where ore was. He was right.

He filed claims. One claim he filed was on some limestone outcrops. He asked an expert miner to evaluate the land and was told it wasn't any good—the mine would be nothing but a humbug. Jesse had faith. The vein found in the mine was one of the richest lead-silver deposits ever found in the West. It was named the Humbug mine.

Jesse found other rich claims, as if some mystic power was leading him to them. At one time he was the largest owner of patented mining properties in the region.

Since Jesse had worked in the rough mining camps back when he was anything but religious, he knew how that atmosphere could affect men and their family lives. He saw men drink away their earnings, leaving their families destitute. He saw men dissipated through vices. He saw men persecuted by peers for trying to live a religious life. He vowed that he would make things different. He built up Knightville, the only mining camp in the West that had no saloons or brothels.

If a miner was caught neglecting his family, he was fired. If a miner was found drunk on the job, he was fired, thus bringing down the rate of accidents in the work place. While other mines worked seven days a week, "Uncle Jesse," as he came to be known, paid his workers more per day and gave them Sundays off. While other mines charged the miners numerous fees for hospital, insurance, education and other services, Uncle Jesse provided benefits to his employees free of charge. Soon there was great unrest in the other mining camps. It was still an era when the American worker was exploited by the extravagantly wealthy mine owners. Miners in other camps began demanding the pay and benefits that Jesse's employees got. Labor unrest threatened. The powerful mining barons decided that they had to do something about Jesse. They had to remove the threat to their own interests. They had to break Jesse somehow.

The mining barons banded together to destroy Uncle Jesse. Smelters that served the mines suddenly refused to smelt ore for Uncle Jesse. Uncle Jesse built his own smelters. Electrical power companies serving the mines refused to sell power to any of Jesse's concerns. Uncle Jesse built his own power lines. Water was cut off.

Uncle Jesse built his own water lines. Coal could no longer be obtained from mines controlled by the mining barons. Uncle Jesse discovered and dug his own coal mine. The local railroads through the mining district suddenly refused to transport Uncle Jesse's ore. Uncle Jesse built his own railroads. Instead of destroying Uncle Jesse, the mining barons forced him to create competing utilities that were more efficient and run by a better-treated, more-willing labor force than their own. Instead of crushing him with their hammer of power, they hit themselves in the head with their own hammer.

To Uncle Jesse, wealth was not a reward arbitrarily gained, it was a responsibility that was given to him. On Uncle Jesse rested the livelihood and welfare of thousands of families. He took that calling seriously.

In 1896, government confiscations and financial sanctions had combined to ruin the Church financially. But the Church could not be broken either. Uncle Jesse was there with money to save the Church in its time of need.

Uncle Jesse created industries to improve the economy of the region and to provide fair employment opportunities to the labor force. He sponsored mills, stores, cattle ranches, irrigation companies. He took a small school in Provo, Utah, named Brigham Young Academy, and endowed it with property, stocks and bonds. The small school, with his gifts, bloomed into a university and is known today as Brigham Young University.

Other than being a home teacher, Uncle Jesse never held a Church job. His was a different calling. His daughter, Inez, and future daughter-in-law, Jennie Brimhall, were the first sister missionaries in the Church to serve full-time missions.

Jesse Knight was revered in his lifetime, not for how much money he made but for how much he gave away. He once said, "The earth is the Lord's bank, and no man has a right to take money out of that bank and use it extravagantly upon himself."

The fortune of the Knight family dwindled and disappeared soon after Uncle Jesse's death in 1921, but he had done with his wealth what he meant to do with it. He had served his calling well and he had made a difference. He was a man who could not be broken.

The Iceberg

The ship was five days out to sea on its journey from Britain to the United States. The passage had been smooth, the open sea illusively calm. But these were the treacherous waters of the North Atlantic.

On August 31, 1899, night descended on the black rolling waves. A murky darkness enveloped the ship. The passengers retired to their beds. Suddenly the stillness of the night was broken by a loud crash. The impact was so great that passengers were thrown from their beds. Furnishings were hurled against bulkheads. Screams and shouts of panic ensued. Those who could peered over the side of the ship. Through the darkness they could make out ice formations jutting up from the sea. The ship had hit an iceberg. The ship, *City of Rome*, and all its passengers, were in peril of their lives.

Thirteen years later, near this very place, another ship, the *Titanic*, would also hit an iceberg. It would also be a dark night. It would also imperil the lives of its passengers. But the similarities would end there.

The *Titanic* was considered unsinkable. The *City of Rome* was accorded no such distinction. The *Titanic* would sink after its collision, taking with it 1,513 lives. The story was different for the collision of the *City of Rome*. Despite the tremendous impact, the crew could discover no serious damage. The integrity of the ship had not been breached. Miraculously, it held.

Among the many passengers on the *City of Rome* that night was a group of twenty-two Latter-day Saints, including missionaries and immigrants. One of the missionaries was a twenty-six-year-old named David. Born in Utah of Scottish immigrants, he was fortunate to have been sent to Scotland to labor among his family's people.

David had just been released from his mission and was on his way home to a small town in Utah.

At home David married and became a teacher, and later, a principal. He served on a Sunday School board. Six-and-a-half years after returning from his mission, in April 1906, David was sitting in the Tabernacle in Salt Lake City, waiting for the concluding address of general conference. President Joseph F. Smith stood and presented the General Authorities of the Church for a sustaining vote. In presenting the Quorum of the Twelve Apostles, he read out the name of the newest apostle—young David.

There was much speculation and amazement among the membership of the Church. It was not just his young age—he was only thirty-two—but he was relatively unknown. He was from a small town, away from the centers of influence. He had never been a bishop. He had never served on a high council. He had never served in a stake presidency. He'd never been ordained a high priest. He had served a two-year mission and held positions of responsibility in the mission field from which, because of a ship's collision with an iceberg, he nearly hadn't returned. And, oh yes, once he had served as a deacons quorum president. That was the astounding sum of his experience. Now he was called to a governing body of the Church.

David served faithfully as an apostle for forty-five years, after which he became Prophet and President of The Church of Jesus Christ of Latter-day Saints. He served in that capacity another eighteen years, during which the Church burst forth with worldwide growth and become an international influence. And much of that growth came through the guidance of the young Scottish missionary, David O. McKay.

The Cripple Who Wanted to Serve a Mission

Members of The Church of Jesus Christ of Latter-day Saints are encouraged to go on missions. But this is the story of a young man who was counseled 'not' to go. He was crippled, and many thought he could not endure the rigors of missionary work.

While he was but a boy, his father gave the young man a blessing which said, ". . . as the Lord designs your salvation and your eternal glory so does the adversary design your destruction." It seems significant that the boy came close to physical destruction many times and survived. Once he was accidentally hit on the head with an ax and survived. Another time he was thrown from a wagon, a wagon wheel passing over his head, and when the team of horses was stopped, they backed up and the wagon wheel again rolled over his head. At age eight he contracted a bone disease. He missed a year of school. He was often in casts and on crutches. The damage done by the disease affected him the rest of his life. At one time he was attacked by a vicious ram, only to be saved by a cast that extended from his shoes to up around his waist. He was stricken with scarlet fever and, later on, by smallpox. He was once buried under a load of hay and again run over by a wagon. None of this dampened his determination to fulfill his purpose in life.

When the young man was 12 years old, he went to a meeting where he heard Elders Alex Bevan and John E. Isgreen bear testimony and tell of their mission experiences. From that time on he did all he could to be worthy of becoming a missionary. It was his dream. He saved his money and studied his scriptures.

At the age of nineteen he was ready for a mission, but again he was on crutches and with a leg cast. He was advised to stay home. So that his lameness would not be held against him, he discarded the crutches and had the leg cast removed. He walked with a limp and with pain that would follow him the rest of his life, but he was determined to show everyone that he could serve a mission. One well-meaning man interceded with church authorities to have the young man's mission deferred, saying he was needed at home. But when the young man found out, he protested and reactivated his mission call. Even one of the elders of the missionary department advised, "It looks to me as if you had better go home and take care of yourself." The young man would have none of it. He wanted to be a missionary!

Finally he reached the mission field—and was assigned an office job in the mission home. But he wanted to preach. After hours, and in his spare time, he went out on his own and preached the gospel.

The young man served his mission. He loved missionary work. So he served another mission. Then he served another mission. Then he served another mission. He spent his life involved in missionary work of one kind or another. Some of his missions were very successful. Others were difficult, and disappointing in terms of the number of investigators who accepted the gospel. Still he preached because of his great love of the Gospel.

By middle age he felt there was a way to preach the gospel to a wider audience, so he wrote a book that he originally entitled "Mormonism." The book sold over two million copies. It went through twenty-three printings. It was translated into eighteen languages including French, Italian, Spanish, Portuguese, Korean, Samoan, Dutch and Thai. It sold more copies than any other Church book outside of the scriptures. The author never took a penny of royalty. He wrote it so he could be a better missionary. Said Elder Thomas S. Monson of the book, "It is a missionary in print."

Elder Sterling W. Still, speaking of contemporary church books other than the scriptures said, "So far as I know, it has been responsible for more converts than all others put together."

Said Elder Richard L. Evans to the author, "I am constantly hearing appreciative, wonderful comments of you and your work, and of the influence that your great book is having in the Church and out of it." The letters of thousands confirm the effectiveness of that book.

The book did not keep its original title. The author, nearing publication, was forcibly impressed by the words of Isaiah from the Bible: "I will proceed to do a marvelous work among this people, even a marvelous work and a wonder." The book *A Marvelous Work and a Wonder* became one of the most influential missionary books of all time and it's author, apostle LeGrand Richards, the crippled boy whom many tried to discourage from serving a mission, became one of the great missionaries of this dispensation.

Bibliography

For More Information:

ATTACK OF THE DEAD CAT
Dalton, Luella Adams, comp. *History of the Iron County Mission.* Parowan, Utah, 1962.

Lucius N. Marsden Family Organization. *William and Lucius N. Marsden—Their History and Posterity.* Provo, UT: Graham Maughn Publishing Company, 1991.

Thornton, William U. "Old Log School House." In *Treasures of Pioneer History*, vol. 1, p. 394. Compiled by Kate Carter. Salt Lake City: Daughters of Utah Pioneers, 1952.

THE BEAR LAKE MONSTERS
Fife, Austin E. "The Bear Lake Monsters." *Utah Humanities Review*, vol. 2. Salt Lake City: University of Utah, 1948.

Paul, J. H. "A Monster Worth While." *Improvement Era.* October 1929, pp. 987-989.

Poulsen, Ezra J. *Joseph C. Rich—Versatile Pioneer.* Salt Lake City: Granite Publishing Company, 1958.

Swarm, Curlohe. "Indian Legend of the Bear Lake Monster." *The Young Woman's Journal.* May 1917, p. 271.

THE BIG MINE
Bingham, Norman F.; Belnap, Lillian B.; Scoville, Lester S., comps. *Sketch of the Life of Erastus Bingham and Family.* Ogden, Utah: Bingham Family Organization, 1953.

"Bingham Shaft to Founder Draws Miners." *Salt Lake Tribune*, 3 August 1949, p. 16.

"Ceremonies Dedicate Shaft Honoring Bingham Family." *Salt Lake Tribune*, 2 August 1949, p. 14.

"Gold is for Paving Streets." *Deseret News*, 5 August 1949, p. 4.

"President George Albert Smith in Charge of Unveiling Bingham Family Marker." *Church News*, 31 July 1949, p. 15.

THE COOPERATIVE CHOIR
Hunt, Duane G. "History of the Roman Catholic Church in Utah." In *Utah—A Centennial History*, p. 691. Edited by Wain Sutton. Salt Lake City: Lewis Historical Publishing Company, 1949.

Kimball, Spencer W. *Conference Reports*, 7 April 1951, p. 177.

Pyper, George D. *Stories of Latter-day Saint Hymns*, p. 83. Salt Lake City: Deseret News Press, 1939.

Silverberg, Robert. *Ghost Towns of the American West*. New York: Thomas Y. Crowell Company, 1968.

THE CRIPPLE WHO WANTED TO SERVE A MISSION
Tate, Lucile C. *LeGrand Richards: Beloved Apostle*. Salt Lake City: Bookcraft, 1982.

THE DEATH PROPHECY
Grant, Heber J. "Word of Wisdom." In *A Story to Tell*, pp. 49-50. Compiled by the General Board of the Primary Association and the Deseret Sunday School Union Board. Salt Lake City: Deseret Book Co., 1945.

Wallis, James H. "President Grant—Defender of the Word of Wisdom." *Improvement Era,* vol. 39 (November 1936), p. 697.

DO YOUR HOMEWORK!
Dedication of the Statue of Philo T. Farnsworth—Proceedings in the Rotunda of the United States Capitol - May 2, 1990. Washington, D.C.: United States Government Printing Office, 199.

Farnsworth, Elma "Pem" G. *Distant Vision.* Salt Lake City: Pemberly Kent Publishers, Inc., 1990.

REVERSE PSYCHOLOGY
Harrington, Judge Daniel. "Pioneer Humor." *Improvement Era,* February 1938, p. 89.

Kimball, J. Golden. *Conference Reports,* April 1906.

Knight, Newell. *Aphorisms, Maxims, Proverbs and Pithy Sayings of Governor Brigham Young Culled From Official Records.* Salt Lake City: Salt Lake City Public Library, 1968.

Valentine, Dan. *The Wit and Wisdom of Brigham Young.* Salt Lake City: American Essays, 1972.

AN EFFECTIVE SPEAKER
Bergera, Gary James and Priddis, Ronald. *Brigham Young University—A House of Faith.* Salt Lake City: Signature Books, 1985.

Holbrook, Raymond Brimhall and Holbrook, Esther Hamilton. *The Tall Pine Tree: The Life and Works of George H. Brimhall.* Salt Lake City: The authors, 1988.

EMERGENCY AT THE VIRGIN DITCH

Bradshaw, Hazel, ed. *Under Dixie Sun.* Panguitch, Utah: Washington County Chapter Daughters of Utah Pioneers, 1950.

Jarvis, Zora Smith, comp. *Sketches from the lives of Brigham Jarvis, Sr. and his wife, Mary Forsythe Jarvis.* St. George, Utah: Zora Smith Jarvis, 1967.

Larson, Andrew Karl. *I Was Called to Dixie.* Salt Lake City: The Deseret News Press, 1961.

EPHRAIM HUMOR

Carter, Kate B. "Three Important Manuscripts." *Daughters of Utah Pioneers Lesson for January.* Salt Lake City: Daughters of Utah Pioneers, 1968.

Cheney, Thomas E. "Scandinavian Immigrant Stories." *Western Folklore,* vol. 18 (April 1959), pp. 99-105.

Jenson, Andrew. *Encyclopedic History of the Church.* Salt Lake City: Deseret News Publishing Company, 1941.

Lee, Hector and Madsen, Royal. "Nicknames of the Ephraimites." *Western Humanities Review,* vol. 3 (January 1949), pp. 12-22.

Mulder, William. "A Sense of Humor - Scandinavian Mormon Immigrant Humor." *The Second Annual Juanita Brooks Lecture.* St. George, Utah: Dixie College, 1985.

West, Orson B. "Denmark—Where Democracy Gives Freedom of Worship." *Improvement Era*, September 1948, pp. 572-573.

ESCAPE FROM LIBERTY

Barrett, Ivan J. *Joseph Smith and the Restoration.* Provo, Utah: Brigham Young University Press, 1973.

"1838 Order of Extermination is Rescinded." *Church News*. 3 July 1976, pp. 4, 13.

Whitman, Dale A. "Extermination Order." In *Encyclopedia of Mormonism*, vol. 2, p. 480. Edited by Daniel H. Ludlow. New York: Macmillan Publishing Company, 1992.

EVICTED FROM THEIR TOWN
Carter, Kate B., comp. "Jefferson County." *Heart Throbs of the West* 7:544-9. Salt Lake City: Daughters of Utah Pioneers, 1939-51.

Scott, Patricia Lyn. *The Hub of Eastern Idaho: a History of Rigby Idaho, 1885-1976*. Caldwell, Idaho: The Caxton Printers, 1976.

FRONTIER M.D.
Arrington, Leonard J. and Madsen, Susan Arrington. *Sunbonnet Sisters*. Salt Lake City: Bookcraft, 1984.

Casterline, Gail Farr. "Dr. Ellis Reynolds Shipp, Pioneer Utah Physician." In *Sister Saints*, pp. 363-82. Edited by Vicky Burgess-Olson. Provo, Utah. Brigham Young University Press, 1973.

"Mormon Women Physicians." *Relief Society Magazine*, August 1915, pp. 345-356.

Noall, Claire. *Guardians of the Hearth*. Bountiful, Utah: Horizon Publishers, 1974.

Richards, Ralph T. *Of Medicine, Hospitals, and Doctors*. Salt Lake City: University of Utah Press, 1953.

Shipp, Ellis Reynolds. *The Early Autobiography and Diary of Ellis Reynolds Shipp, M.D.* Salt Lake City: Deseret News Press, 1962.

Skalla, Judy. "Beloved Healer." In *The Women Who Made the West*, pp. 152-63. The Western Writers of America. Garden City, N.Y.: Doubleday, 1981.

GHOST IN THE PICTURE

Arrington, Leonard J. *Brigham Young: American Moses.* New York: Alfred A. Knopf, 1985.

Lester, Margaret D. *Brigham Street.* Salt Lake City: Utah State Historical Society, 1979.

Young, S. Dilworth. *Here is Brigham.* Salt Lake City: Bookcraft, 1964.

THE GOSPEL ACCORDING TO GIBSON

Carter, Kate B., ed. *Our Pioneer Heritage.* vol. 6. Salt Lake City: Daughters of Utah Pioneers, 1963.

"Confounding the Wise." In *Junior Classes Manual*, pp. 44-7. Salt Lake City: The General Board of Y.M.M.I.A., 1922.

Journal History, 5 January 1875, p. 2.

HALF A WORLD AWAY

Hartshorn, Leon R., comp. *Outstanding Stories by General Authorities*, pp. 172-178. Salt Lake City: Deseret Book Co., 1970.

Simpson, Robert L. "The Lord is Mindful of His Own." *BYU Speeches of the Year*, 4 April 1962.

HE COULDN'T BE BROKEN

Knight, Jesse William. *The Jesse Knight Family.* Salt Lake City: The Deseret News Press, 1940.

Mangum, Diane L. "Jesse Knight and the Riches of Life." *Ensign*, October 1993, pp. 54-59.

Whitney, Orson F. *History of Utah*, vol. 4. Salt Lake City: George Q. Cannon and Sons, 1904.

HEALING STONES
Ritchie, Cora Carver. "The Wooden Doll." In *A Story to Tell*, pp. 368-71. Compiled by the General Board of the Primary Association and the Deseret Sunday School Union Board. Salt Lake City: Deseret Book Co., 1945.

HEAVENLY FIRST AID
Watson, Elden Jay, ed. *Manuscript History of Brigham Young, 1802-1844.* Salt Lake City: Smith Secretarial Service, 1968.

Wells, Emmeline B. "Biography of Mary Ann Angell Young." *Juvenile Instructor.* 15 January 1891, p. 57.

HERO FOR PEACE
Bozic, Marinko. "Mormon Shadow Falls Over Sportsman." *Vecernje Novosti* (Belgrade, Yugoslavia), 9 July 1975. Translation in Church Historical Department.

Jenkins, Carri P. "He Seeks Winning Game Plan for Peace." *Church News*, 9 January 1993, p. 7.

"Hall of Fame Honors Former BYU Standout." *Church News*, 10 February 1996, p. 4.

HE SPOKE WITH HUMOR AND PERSUASIVE POWER
Nibley, Preston. *The Presidents of the Church.* Salt Lake City: Deseret Book Company, 1974.

"Proceedings of a Testimonial to Heber C. Kimball and Thomas S. Williams." Testimonial was held at Liberty Park, Salt Lake City, June 14, 1940, Quince K. Kimball being in charge.

Roberts, B. H. *History of the Church*. Salt Lake City: Deseret Book Company, 1932.

Roberts, B. H. *The Life of John Taylor*. Salt Lake City: George Q. Cannon and Sons Company, 1892.

THE ICEBERG

Gibbons, Francis M. *David O. McKay: Apostle to the World, Prophet of God*. Salt Lake City: Deseret Book Co., 1986.

J. GOLDEN AND THE BRASS BAND

Arrington, James W. *J. Golden.* (sound recording) Salt Lake City: Covenant Recordings, 1983.

Cheney, Thomas Ed. *The Golden Legacy*. Santa Barbara and Salt Lake City: Peregrine Smith, Inc., 1974.

Conference Reports of The Church of Jesus Christ of Latter-day Saints.

Richards, Claude. *J. Golden Kimball: The Story of a Unique Personality*. Salt Lake City: Bookcraft, 1966.

Roberts, B. H. "The Tennessee Massacre." *Contributor*, 6 October 1884, pp. 16-23.

JAPANESE LAND

Benson, Lee. "Tokyo Temple to Rise on Historic Site." *Church News*, 2 September 1978, p. 14.

Britsch, R. Lanier. "The Blossoming of the Church in Japan." *Ensign*, October 1992, pp. 32-38.

Cowley, Matthew. *Conference Reports*, 30 September 1949, pp. 46-47.

Nelson, Terry G. *The History of the Church of Jesus Christ of Latter-day Saints in Japan from 1948 to 1980.* Masters thesis, Brigham Young University, 1986.

Smith, Henry A. *Matthew Cowley—Man of Faith.* Salt Lake City: Bookcraft, 1954.

THE KID WHO DROVE CARS
O'Brien, Robert. *Marriott.* Salt Lake City: Deseret Book Company, 1979.

"Philanthropist J. Willard Marriott Dies at 84." *Church News*, 18 August 1985, pp. 7, 16.

LIVELY SPIRITS
Jenson, Andrew. *Latter-day Saint Biographical Encyclopedia*, 4 vols. Salt Lake City: Andrew Jenson History Company, 1901-1936.

Whitney, Orson F. *Through Memory's Halls*. Independence, Missouri: Zion's Printing and Publishing Company, 1930.

THE MAN WHO GOT COAL FOR CHRISTMAS
Gibbons, Francis M. *George Albert Smith—Kind and Caring Christian; Prophet of God.* Salt Lake City: Deseret Book Company, 1990.

Stewart, Emily Smith. "Christmas at Our House." In *A Story to Tell*, pp. 460-465. Compiled by General Board of the Primary Assoc.

and the Deseret Sunday School Union Board. Salt Lake City: Deseret Book Company, 1945.

MAORI PROPHECY

Cowley, Matthew. "Maori Chief Predicts Coming of LDS Missionaries." *Improvement Era*, September 1950, pp. 696-698, 754-756.

Cowley, Matthew. *Matthew Cowley Speaks*. Salt Lake City: Deseret Book Company, 1976.

Hunt, Brian W. *Zion in New Zealand*. Temple View, New Zealand: Church College of New Zealand, 1977.

A MODERN WOMAN

Arrington, Leonard J. and Madsen, Susan Arrington. *Sunbonnet Sisters*, pp. 117-125. Salt Lake City: Bookcraft, 1984.

Bennion, Sherilyn Cox. *Equal to the Occasion*. Reno: University of Nevada Press, 1990.

Richards, Lula Green. *Branches That Run Over the Wall*. Salt Lake City: The Magazine Printing Company, 1904.

Richards, Lula Green. "Valedictory." *Woman's Exponent*, 1 October 1877, p. 36.

Romney, Thomas C. "Louisa Lula Greene Richards." *Instructor*, September 1950, pp. 262-263.

MONUMENT TO DREAMS

Fite, Gilbert C. *Mount Rushmore*. Norman, Oklahoma: University of Oklahoma Press, 1952.

Jensen, Richard L. *The Mormon Years of the Borglum Family—Task Papers in L.D.S. History*, No. 26. Salt Lake City: Historical

Department of The Church of Jesus Christ of Latter-day Saints, 1979.

Zeitner, June Culp and Borglum, Lincoln. *Borglum's Unfinished Dream—Mount Rushmore.* Aberdeen, South Dakota: North Plains Press, 1976.

MUSICAL IDENTITY

Klopfer, W. Herbert. "Enemy Soldier at the Pulpit." *Ensign*, June 1990, pp. 59-60.

"New Board Members." *Church News*, 27 January 1996, p. 12.

VanOrden, LaVonne, comp. *Blessed by the Hymns.* Salt Lake City: Deseret Book Company, 1989.

THE MYSTERIOUS SUBSTANCE

Kretchman, Herbert F. *The Story of Gilsonite.* Salt Lake City: American Gilsonite Company, 1957.

McGraw-Hill Encyclopedia of Science and Technology, 7th ed. New York: McGraw-Hill. Inc., 1992.

THE NAUGHTY BOY

Anderson, James H. "George Q. Cannon." *Juvenile Instructor*, 15 January 1900, pp. 33-40.

Cannon Family Historical Treasury. Salt Lake City: George Cannon Family Association, 1967.

Sauls, Elizabeth Cannon. *The Life of George Q. Cannon.* Provo, Utah, 1956.

A NEW TREND

"Developer Sidney M. Horman Dies." *Deseret News*, 31 December 1995.

"Foundation Honors Seven Heroes." *Church News*, 4 March 1995, p. 6.

"Realtors Name Citizen of the Year." *Deseret News*, 22 January 1980.

NO PLACE TO LOSE A COW

Bradshaw, Hazel, ed. *Under Dixie Sun*. Panguitch, Utah:Washington County Chapter Daughters of Utah Pioneers, 1950.

Larson, A. Karl and Larson, Katharine Miles, eds. *Diary of Charles Lowell Walker*. Logan, Utah: Utah State University Press, 1980.

Orden, Dell Van. "Members Answer Calls to Colonize Despite Hardships." *Church News*, 26 May 1979, p. 4.

THE NON-MORMON WHO SAVED NAUVOO

"A Glimpse of the Past." *Deseret Evening News*, 20 October 1888, p. 2.

Avery, Valeen Tippetts and Newell, Linda King. "Lewis C. Bidamon, Stepchild of Mormondom." *Brigham Young University Studies,* vol. 19 (Spring 1979), pp. 375-388.

Committee in Behalf of the New Citizens. Broadside circular signed by fifty non-Mormon citizens of Nauvoo including L.C. Bidamon, 1846. Church Historical Dept.

Jenson, Andrew, and Stevenson, Edward. *Infancy of the Church*. Salt Lake City, 1889.

Jenson, Andrew. *L.D.S. Biographical Encyclopedia*, vol. 1. Salt Lake City: The Andrew Jenson History Co., 1901.

Mower, Nathalie. "Bidamon Sisters Become Members." *Church News*, 22 October 1977, p. 10.

PARLEY AND THE BULL DOG
Pratt, Parley P. *Autobiography of Parley Parker Pratt.* Salt Lake City: Deseret Book Company, 1964.

Stanley, Reva. *The Archer of Paradise.* Caldwell, Idaho: The Caxton Printers, LTD., 1937.

PLAYING WITH GUNS
Browning, John and Gentry, Curt. *John M. Browning, American Gunmaker.* Garden City, New York: Doubleday, 1964.

Johnson, Allen and Malone, Dumas. *Dictionary of American Biography.* New York: Charles Scribner's Sons, 1958.

"The Greatest Inventor of Guns in the World." *Current Opinion*, July 1918, pp. 20-21.

Van Leer, Twila. "Utah Gunsmith's Ingenuity Was No Flash in the Pan." *Deseret News*, 20 February 1996, pp. B1-B2.

THE PROMISED BABE
Arrington, Leonard J. and Madsen, Susan Arrington. *Mothers of the Prophets.* Salt Lake City: Deseret Book Company, 1987.

Gibbons, Francis M. *Harold B. Lee: Man of Vision, Prophet of God.* Salt Lake City: Deseret Book Company, 1993.

Goates, L. Brent. *Harold B. Lee: Prophet and Seer.* Salt Lake City: Bookcraft, 1985.

Young, S. Dilworth. "Having Been Born of Goodly Parents." *New Era*. March 1973, pp. 4-8.

PUT THEM RIGHT

Durham, G. Homer. *N. Eldon Tanner: His Life and Service*. Salt Lake City: Deseret Book Company, 1982.

Tanner, N. Eldon. "My Experiences and Observations." *BYU Speeches of the Year*. May 17, 1966, pp. 6-7.

Tanner, Maurice, comp. *John Tanner Family*. Salt Lake City: The Tanner Family Association, 1942.

REBEL WITH A CAUSE

Cornwall, J. Spencer. *Stories of our Mormon Hymns*. Salt Lake City: Deseret Book Company, 1975.

Davidson, Karen Lynn. *Our Latter-day Hymns*. Salt Lake City: Deseret Book Company, 1988.

Leiper, Maria and Simon, Henry W. *A Treasury of Hymns*. New York: Simon and Schuster, 1953.

Pyper, George D. *Stories of Latter-day Hymns*. Salt Lake City: Deseret News Press, 1939.

THE RED GHOST

Arizona State Teachers College of Flagstaff, spons. *Arizona—State Guide*. New York: Hastings House Publishers, 1941.

Farish, Thomas Edwin. *History of Arizona*, vol. 1. Phoenix: Thomas Farish, 1915.

Roberts, B. H. *A Comprehensive History of the Church*, vol. 4. Salt Lake City: Deseret News Press, 1930.

Robertson, Frank C. and Harris, Beth Kay. *Boom Towns of the Great Basin*. Denver: Sage Books, 1962.

Trimble, Marshall. *Arizona—A Panoramic History of a Frontier State*. Garden City, NY: Doubleday and Company, 1977.

THE RUNAWAY

Cowley, Matthew. *Matthew Cowley Speaks*. Salt Lake City: Deseret Book Co., 1976.

Cowley, Matthew. *Conference Report*. 5 October 1945, p. 50.

"Matthias F. Cowley Taken By Death." *Improvement Era*, July 1940, p. 414.

Smith, Henry A. *Matthew Cowley—Man of Faith*. Salt Lake City: Bookcraft, 1954.

Stout, Wayne. *History of Utah*. vol. 2. Salt Lake City: Wayne Stout, 1968.

SANTA CLAUS VERSUS THE KU KLUX KLAN

Alexander, Thomas G. and Allen, James B. *Mormons and Gentiles*. Boulder, Colorado: Pruett Publishing Company, 1984.

Gerlach, Larry R. *Blazing Crosses in Zion: The Ku Klux Klan in Utah*. Logan, Utah: Utah State University Press, 1982.

"S. L. Ku Klux Unmasks Santa Claus—Protest Brings Order to Police." *Salt Lake Telegram*, 23 December 1925, p. 1.

"Santa Must Cut Out the Mask or Quit the Street." *Salt Lake Telegram*, 24 December 1925, p. 18.

SUPER STAR

"Choir Greeted By Miss Maude Adams." *Salt Lake Tribune*, 12 November 1911, p. 1.

Kiskadden, Annie Adams and Porter, Verne Hardin. "The Life Story of Maude Adams and Her Mother." *The Green Book Magazine*, June 1914.

Melville, James Keith. *The Mormon Drama and Maude Adams*. Provo, Utah: Brigham Young University, Division of Continuing Education, 1965.

Pearson, Howard. "Utah's Maude Adams Inspires a Romantic Fantasy." *Deseret News*, 23 September 1980, p. C7.

Pyper, George D. *The Romance of an Old Playhouse*. Salt Lake City: Deseret News Press, 1937.

Whitney, Orson F. *Through Memory's Halls*. Independence, Missouri: Zion's Printing and Publishing Company, 1930.

TALE OF THE BUCKSKIN PANTS

Fisher, Margaret M. *Utah and the Civil War*. Salt Lake City: Deseret Book Company, 1929.

Whitney, Orson F. *History of Utah*, vol. 2. Salt Lake City: George Q. Cannon and Sons Company, Publishers, 1893.

TALE OF THE DEAD COYOTE

Drake, J. Raman. *Howard Egan, Frontiersman, Pioneer and Pony Express Rider*. Masters thesis, Brigham Young University, 1956.

Knighton, Doris. "Major Egan and the Coyote." In *Treasures of Pioneer History*, pp. 379-380. Compiled by Kate Carter. Salt Lake City: Daughters of Utah Pioneers, 1952.

Lambert, Darwin. *Great Basin Drama*. Niwot, Colorado: Roberts Rinehart Publishers, 1991.

Nibley, Preston W. "Howard Egan Was Member of Original Group of Pioneers." *Church News*, 30 October 1954, p. 16.

TATERS AND TESTIMONY
"Deaths." *Church News*, 14 January 1995, p. 10.

"F. N. Grigg, Founder of Ore-Ida, Dies." *Deseret News*, 8 January 1995, p. B7.

Grigg, F. Nephi. "Living in the World Without Being Part of the World." *Improvement Era*, October 1966, p. 934.

Johnson, Cleo Grigg. *Five Generations of Mormonism—A Grigg Family Genealogy*. Salt Lake City: Deseret News Press, 1956.

TEST OF BROTHERHOOD
"Basketball Invitation Led Hesitant Youth to Church." *Church News*, 30 November 1991, p. 10.

Gibbons, Francis M. *David O. McKay, Apostle to the World, Prophet of God*. Salt Lake City: Deseret Book Company, 1986.

Nelson, Terry G. *The History of The Church of Jesus Christ of Latter-day Saints in Japan from 1948-1980*. Masters Thesis, Brigham Young University, 1986.

Rodriguez, Derin Head. *From Every Nation*. Salt Lake City: Deseret Book Company, 1990.

THAT FACE
"Colleen Kay Hutchins, Miss America of 1952." *Listen—A Journal of Better Living*, April-June 1952, p. 5.

Green, Doyle L. "Colleen Hutchins—Miss America 1952." *Improvement Era*, June 1952, pp. 396-397, 464-466.

King, Walter. "Queen of Beauty." *Allied Youth*, September 1952, p. 2.

THE UNLOVED WOMAN

Burgess-Olsen, Vicky, ed. *Sister Saints*. Provo, UT: Brigham Young University Press, 1973.

Eaton-Gadsby, Patricia Rasmussen and Dushku, Judith Rasmussen. "I Have Risen Triumphant." In *Sister Saints*, pp. 455-480. Provo, UT: Brigham Young University Press, 1973.

"The Gull Monument." *Improvement Era,* vol. 17 (November 1913), p. 65.

Madsen, Carol Cornwall. "Emmeline B. Wells: Romantic Rebel." In *Supporting Saints*, pp. 305-41. Provo, UT: Brigham Young University Religious Studies Center, 1985.

Madsen, Carol Cornwall. *A Mormon Woman in Victorian America*. Ph. D. dissertation. University of Utah, 1985.

Peterson, Janet, and Gaunt, LaRene. *Elect Ladies*. Salt Lake City: Deseret Book Co., 1990.

"President and Mrs. Wilson Make Informal Call on Aged Leader, 'Aunt Em' Wells." *Deseret Evening News*, 24 September 1919, p. 11.

Wells, Emmeline B. *Emmeline B. Wells Diary*. Provo, UT: Special Collections, Harold B. Lee Library, Brigham Young University.

Wells, Emmeline B. "The Mission of Saving Grain." *Relief Society Magazine*, 2 February 1915, p. 47.

THE UNPOPULAR GIRL

Arrington, Leonard J. and Madsen, Susan Arrington. *Sunbonnet Sisters*. Salt Lake City: Bookcraft, 1984.

History of Kane County. Salt Lake City: Kane County Daughters of Utah Pioneers, 1970.

Kane, Joseph Nathan. *Famous First Facts*, 4th ed. New York: H. W. Wilson Company, 1981.

Mary E. Woolley Chamberlain: Handmaiden of the Lord. Provo, Utah: published by the family, 1981?

THE UNUSUAL SPEAKER

Blue, Chief Samuel and Smith, George Albert. *Conference Reports*, April 1950, pp. 141-143.

"Chief Blue's Testimony." *Church News*, 10 October 1981, p. 24.

"Faith." *New Era-Young Women Special Issue*, November 1985, pp. 28-29.

Journal History. 29 July 1908, p. 9.

A WILD WEST TALE

"Buffalo Bill Enjoyed Going on an 1893 Utah Deer Hunt." *Deseret News*, 20 October 1980, p. A12.

Johnson, Allen and Malone, Dumas. *Dictionary of American Biography*. New York: Charles Scribner's Sons, 1958.

Russell, Don. *The Lives and Legends of Buffalo Bill*. Norman, Oklahoma: University of Oklahoma Press, 1973.